TEXAS
CURIOSITIES

TEXAS

CURIOSITIES

QUIRKY CHARACTERS,
ROADSIDE ODDITIES
& OFFBEAT FUN

JOHN KELSO

Revised by Paris Permenter
and John Bigley

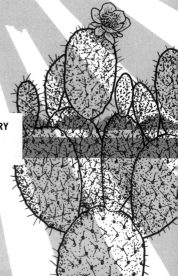

Globe
Pequot
GUILFORD, CONNECTICUT

Thanks to our dogs Irie and Tiki who traveled the backroads with us and resisted the temptation to chase what just might be the world's biggest squirrel and bravely posed beneath the world's biggest blue crab without a bark.

–PARIS PERMENTER AND JOHN BIGLEY

Thanks to my Kay, and my daughter, Rachel, for keeping me smiling, providing inspiration, and laughing at my jokes and weird sound effects. And yes, Rachel, I'll enter the Shamrock beard contest if you'll clean up your room.

—JOHN KELSO

Globe
Pequot

An imprint of The Rowman & Littlefield Publishing Group, Inc.
4501 Forbes Blvd., Ste. 200
Lanham, MD 20706
www.rowman.com

Distributed by NATIONAL BOOK NETWORK

British Library Cataloguing in Publication Information available

Library of Congress Cataloging-in-Publication Data available

ISBN 978-1-4930-2369-1 (paperback)
ISBN 978-1-4930-2370-7 (e-book)

∞™ The paper used in this publication meets the minimum requirements of American National Standard for Information Sciences—Permanence of Paper for Printed Library Materials, ANSI/NISO Z39.48-1992.

Printed in the United States of America

All the information in this guidebook is subject to change. We recommend you call ahead to obtain current information before traveling.

Contents

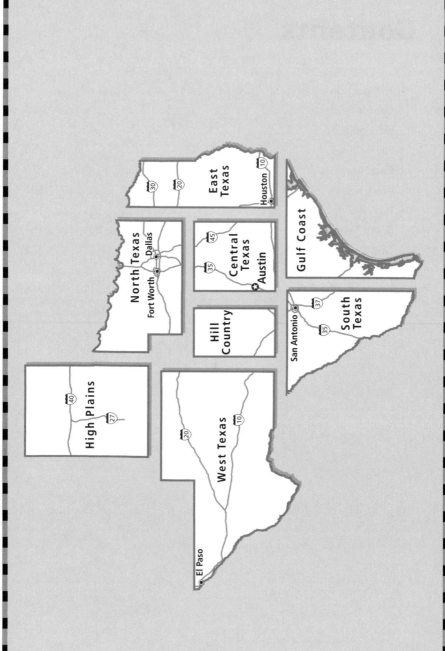

Texas

Introduction

You know Texas for the Alamo, the theme parks, the Texas-sized malls, the miles of beaches. But even for long-time travelers to the Lone Star State, there are plenty of attractions you just might have missed. Have you examined the world's largest killer bee? Stood within the eternal Stonehenge circle? Told your fish story beside the world's largest rod and reel? From the deserts of West Texas to the piney woods of the eastern reaches of the state, you'll find plenty of unique and unusual attractions in Texas including some that are just downright quirky.

Of course, in a state where bigger is better, you sometimes have to be *really* big to get attention. Across the Lone Star State, travelers find more than the usual share of gargantuan statues, perfect backdrops for a family vacation photo.

We've walked the path set forth by John Kelso, updating this book filled with sometimes quirky, sometimes funny, sometimes puzzling, but always amusing destinations. As with all travel guides, *Texas Curiosities* is just a guide, a roadmap from which to start your own explorations. Keep an eye out for the biggest, smallest, oldest, weirdest, and just plain head-shaking attractions as you explore this one-of-a-kind state that is Texas.

—PARIS PERMENTER AND JOHN BIGLEY

Texas Curiosities Hall of Fame

Well, here we go again, updating *Texas Curiosities*, a book that has taken on a life of its own.

Speaking of that, we've suffered some sad losses in the *Texas Curiosities* family in this, the fourth redo (fifth edition) of this book. Some of my favorite curiosities have gone toes up, so we've had to remove them from these pages. Each time one of these places disappears, it's kind of like losing a crazy uncle.

Which has led me to come up with the *Texas Curiosities* Hall of Fame.

To make it into the Hall, the *Texas Curiosities* item has to have ceased to exist and have left behind a treasured legacy. The idea is to honor posthumorously those quirky museums, folks, vacation spots, or whatever that used to be featured in this book but are no longer with us.

You probably thought I meant to say "posthumously," but because of the nature of this silly travelogue, I figure posthumorously fits the story line better. Sadly these attractions have gone on to the big guidebook in the sky:

The Cockroach Hall of Fame Museum, Plano: The museum consisted of about two dozen little three-dimensional scenes that featured dead celebrity roaches dressed in costumes on display, appropriately enough, at a pest control business. The exhibits, the winners in a nationwide contest, were quite elaborate. The Liberoachi scene featured a dead roach sitting at a toy piano decorated with a tiny candelabra. Liberoachi was wearing a white cape. The diorama even played music. Then there was the Combates Motel, a take-off on the Bates Motel in the Hitchcock movie *Psycho*. This tiny roach-sized house featured a roach carrying an itsy-bitsy dagger. As proof that there's a buyer for just about everything, the Cockroach Hall of Fame Museum is no longer in the book because it has been sold and moved out of state.

Forbidden Gardens, Katy: The park included thousands of terra-cotta soldier replicas crafted to look like the ones dug up about one and a half miles from the tomb of Emperor Qin, who ruled China in the third century BC. Sadly the attraction was closed due to a highway expansion.

Paseo del Rio Mud Festival, San Antonio. The Paseo del Rio Mud Festival—as the name implies—was held on the swanky River Walk, the most visited tourist attraction in Texas. Alas, the mud slinging has come to an end.

Spamarama, Austin: An outlandish spoof of the traditional Texas chili cook-off, this annual rite was held early each spring featuring every conceivable Spam dish: Spamwurst, Spamchiladas, Spambo (Spam gumbo), Spamalama Ding Dongs, moo goo gai Spam, chicken-fried Spam, Spamachini Alfredo, piggy pâté, and even Spamish fly, a Waldorf salad in which the raisins served as the flies.

But life goes on, and we've found enough new material to take the places of those we've left behind. So sit back in the passenger seat and join me once again as we romp around the Lone Star State looking for goofy stuff. I'll drive, and you watch the map.

—JOHN KELSO

Central Texas

"Keep Austin Weird" is the unofficial motto of the largest city in Central Texas. Hmm… was that any of John Kelso's doing? Anyway, you'll see it on T-shirts and bumper stickers all over Austin. Folks seem genuinely proud of their weirdness; there's even a Museum of the Weird. In the rest of the state, the bumper stickers say "Keep the Weirdos in Austin." Seems fair enough.

Austin, Texas's state capital and home to the University of Texas, is a vibrant cultural center full of college students, musicians, artists, and technology geeks. As the Live Music Capital of the World, it boasts more than 250 music venues, so you can find live music every night of the week.

The state-of-the-art Bullock Texas State History Museum is second to none and a great way to learn about the Lone Star State. Austin offers prime outdoor recreation venues, including three lakes, dozens of parks, a nature center, swimming pools, botanical gardens, and miles of surfaced hike and bike pathways along greenbelts and lakes.

However, not all the oddities of Central Texas are in Austin. The rolling hills of Central Texas, a transitional area between the plains of West Texas and the piney woods of East Texas, contain countless small Texas towns with their own stories and quirky characters. I-35 runs basically north–south through Central Texas, so most folks hurry by and miss some of the delightful small towns along the way.

Wander through the largest outlet shopping mall in Texas (more than 250 shops) in San Marcos. Splash in the world's first water resort at Schlitterbahn in New Braunfels. Waco, another bustling city in this region, is home to Baylor University and the Texas Ranger Hall of Fame Museum (lawmen, not baseball players), as well as the drugstore where Dr Pepper was invented.

Hey, Abbott!
Abbott

No, this town a couple miles off I-35 (FM 1242) with a population of about 300 people is not located next to Costello.

Don't come here looking for Willie Nelson stuff, even though the music giant has a house here and visits occasionally when he isn't on the road (again). The town has no Willie Nelson T-shirt shops and just a street sign that

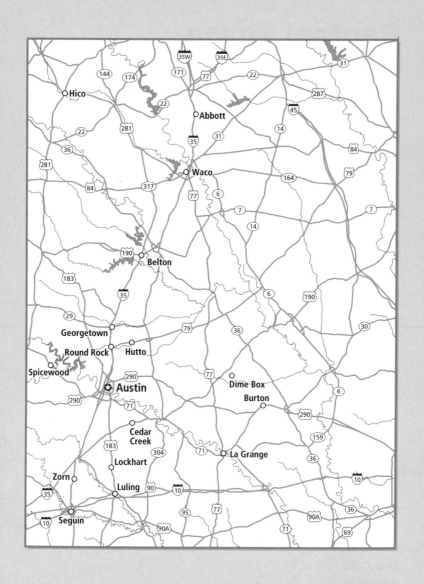

Central Texas

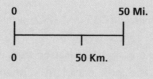

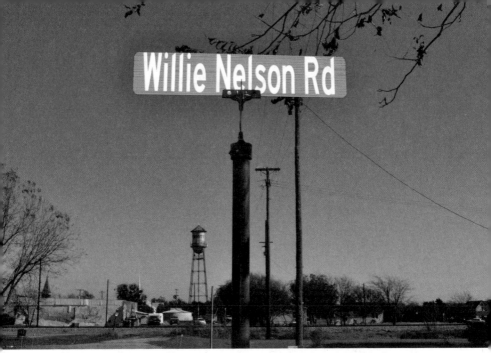

This street sign confirms that, yes, Abbott is the hometown of Willie Nelson.

bears his name. There used to be a billboard out near I-35 that had his face on it, but it's long gone.

"That's exactly the way he wants it," said former school superintendent Terry Timmons.

If you go by the high school, you can track down the 1950 high school yearbook and find Willie in it, although in the book Nelson is referred to as Willie Hugh Nelson. Willie graduated from Abbott High in 1950. By thumbing through the book, you'll find young Mister Nelson was a pretty busy and versatile kid.

He was number 15 on the football team. The yearbook shows a photo of Willie with his arm cocked, ready to toss a pass. He played baseball and volleyball; was a guard on the basketball team; ran track; worked a couple years on *The Spotlight*, the school newspaper; and, not surprisingly, was the Future Farmers of America song leader.

When Willie comes to town, it's no big deal to the locals—or to him, either. He's just one of the neighbors.

"Unless you see him or his pickup, you don't know he's here," Timmons said.

The O. Henry Pun-Off World Championships
Austin

"The best kind are the kind where somebody comes up with something off the top of their head that's almost too good to come off the top of your head," said Gary Hallock, master puntificator and man in charge of Austin's annual groanathon.

An example? The subject was religion, and the punsters had to address that subject in pun. The competitor made up a quote as if it were coming from Nancy Reagan. "The problems with the economy? They're all Deuteronomy," the punster said.

Due to Ron and me. Get it?

The annual event, usually held on a Saturday in early-to-mid May in honor of short-story writer O. Henry, began in 1977 and attracts large crowds. "They just keep coming back because everybody is so annual retentive, you see," Hallock explained. "The throngs get larger each year, but we don't want more than one throng every year because two throngs don't make a right."

Punsters can compete in two events. In Punniest of Show, entrants get ninety seconds to do a prearranged program. In Punslingers, punsters square

Even if you can't make the Pun-Off, O. Henry's home makes a fun stop.
PARIS PERMENTER AND JOHN BIGLEY

off against each other two at a time. They're given a topic at random, and they get five seconds to come up with a pun on the subject. When you come up punless, you're through. The last punster standing wins.

The capital city of Texas is the perfect spot for this event, since, being the home of the University of Texas, it's full of smart-asses and intellectuals—self-proclaimed or otherwise. "Austin is a mecca for punsters," Hallock explained. "So sooner or later you've got to get down here so you can meet your mecca."

This doesn't mean you have to be a punster to come and enjoy the program. "We don't mind people who are not punsters in the audience because we can enroll you in our Witless Protection Program," Hallock said.

Glutton for punishment? Call the O. Henry Museum at (512) 472-1903 or try punoff.com.

Museum of the Weird
Austin

Any Texan knows the Museum of the Weird could only be in Austin (museumoftheweird.com; 412 E. Sixth St., 512-476-5493). Claiming to be the "Weirdest Show on Earth," this place is stuffed with a strange collection of oddities, like freaks of nature, monsters, mummies, giant lizards, shrunken heads, unexplained phenomena, and the supernatural.

It all resides in the back of Steve Busti's store, the Lucky Lizard Curios and Gifts, which features such items as the book *Monsters of Texas* and the DVD *Southern Fried Bigfoot*. Other offerings include one-of-a-kind gifts, souvenir shrunken heads, ghost books, and "Keep Austin Weird" T-shirts and hats.

The Museum of the Weird does its part to Keep Austin Weird.
PARIS PERMENTER AND JOHN BIGLEY

Mexican Free-Tailed Bat Colony
Austin

What critter has the biggest population living under the Ann W. Richards Congress Avenue Bridge? Before 1980, if you had answered "wino" to that question, you would have been right.

In 1980, construction on the bridge created a crevice 18 inches deep and 3⁄4 to 11⁄2 inches wide, the perfect size for pregnant bats to hang out in and give birth. In the summer, 1.5 million bats live under the bridge, making it North America's largest urban bat colony. The bats can consume up to fifteen tons of insects a night, according to Arnie Phifer, formerly of Bat Conservation International, an organization based in Austin.

When the bats emerge from under the bridge at sundown, tourists flock to watch at a bat-viewing area near the bridge on the south shore of Lady Bird Lake. Bat Conservation International has a "bat hotline" (512) 327-9721) that provides bat updates. Or check out their website: batcon.org.

The bat colony has caused a lot of batphernalia to spring up around Austin. The city has a bat statue, which turns in the wind, near the bridge. When there was a Saks Fifth Avenue located in Austin, the swank store used to sell an Austin snow globe—shake the globe and instead of snow, tiny bats flew about. The Austin Public Library's Youth Program has a performing rock band named Echo and the Bats featuring songs based on popular children's books.

It's a bird, it's a plane...no, it's a whole bunch of bats. PARIS PERMENTER AND JOHN BIGLEY

Moonlight Towers
Austin

Austin is the only city in the world that has surviving moonlight towers. Scattered around town, most are in "old" Austin around the Capitol.

Moonlight towers were popular in the late nineteenth century in cities across the United States and Europe. At 165 feet tall (150 feet of tower and 15 feet of foundation) with six gigantic lamps, they were designed to emit enough light to illuminate an area of several blocks at night. Austin purchased thirty-one used towers from Detroit in 1894. Rumor had it that the lights were installed as a defense against the Servant Girl Annihilator, a serial murderer who killed eight people and attacked another eight. In reality, the towers were erected a decade after the Central Texas predecessor of Jack the Ripper terrorized the capital city.

Original carbon-arc lamps were replaced with incandescent lamps at that time and then with mercury-vapor lamps in the 1930s. A central switch

"Yule" really love this moonlight tower. PARIS PERMENTER AND JOHN BIGLEY

was installed during World War II so all the lamps could be turned off in case of a blackout. Eventually, as street lights became more common, the moonlight towers began to disappear.

In 1993, the city of Austin dismantled its remaining seventeen towers (of the original thirty-one) and restored every piece down to each bolt in time for their 100th anniversary. When completed, the huge undertaking was celebrated with a citywide festival. One of Austin's most famous movies, *Dazed and Confused*, star Matthew McConaughey utters the line for which the towers will always be known: "Party at the Moon Tower."

The seventeen remaining towers were listed in the National Register of Historic Places in 1976 and are also Texas Archeological Landmarks. The most visible is the tower in Zilker Park which is transformed, with the addition of hundreds of lights, into the annual Zilker Park Christmas Tree.

The (Almost) Shortest Highway in Texas and the Texas State Cemetery
Austin

At 0.90 mile, TX 165 is the second shortest state highway in Texas, after TX 168 in Galveston, which is 0.87 mile. Who would quibble over 0.03 mile? I'll bet TX 165 is the only one locked at night, though, as it runs through the Texas State Cemetery, where the speed limit is a mere ten miles per hour.

TX 165 is one of the state's most unique (and quickest) road trips.
PARIS PERMENTER AND JOHN BIGLEY

You can drive or walk along the cemetery road seven days a week between 8:00 a.m. and 5:00 p.m., but the Texas State Cemetery Visitor Center, where you can see exhibits of Texas history and/or arrange a free guided tour, is open Monday through Friday, 8:00 a.m. to 5:00 p.m. You can walk among such famous folks as Stephen F. Austin, John Connolly, Bob Bullock, Tom Landry, J. Frank Dobie, and James Michener.

It's the final resting place for more than 2,200 Confederate soldiers, thirteen governors, thirty Texas Rangers, and veterans of every war as far back as the Revolutionary War—yes, 1776. A monument to September 11, 2001, stands tall, as does one dedicated to hundreds of Tennessee teenagers who came to fight for Texas independence.

If you can't visit, check out the website at cemetery.state.tx.us. It's interactive, so you can search by name or location and read biographies of the residents and learn lots of history.

Robotic Politician
Austin

Think politicians all-too-often sound like robots? Well, at The Lyndon Baines Johnson Library and Museum, also known as the LBJ Presidential Library,

LBJ, stand up Comedian-in-Chief. PARIS PERMENTER AND JOHN BIGLEY

one animatronic president may be standing at a podium but he doesn't spout political rhetoric—he cracks jokes.

The life-sized LBJ, surrounded by political cartoons, is the star of the show in the Humor and the Presidency exhibit on the ground floor of the library. The stories are ones that LBJ often told at dinners, and visitors can hear the sound of laughter as the thirty-sixth President recounts stories like the one of a Hill Country man who went to the doctor because he couldn't hear. The physician asked him how much he drank a day; he said about a pint. The doctor explained that he'd have to cut out drinking to improve his hearing.

Ninety days went by and the man went back to the doctor, still unable to hear. The doctor asked if he'd cut out drinking. He answered no. The doctor explained that he couldn't help if he wouldn't follow instructions. The answer: "Well doctor, I got home and I considered it. And I just decided that I like what I drank much better than what I heard."

Cochran, Blair & Potts
Belton

Commonly, ancient stores have dusty inventories to match their long histories. But Cochran, Blair & Potts, the oldest department store in Texas, located at 221 E. Central in Belton is actually a working business. Hey, it ain't Saks, but they do have Red Wing shoes. Ironically, the store is located near the Area Agency on Aging of Central Texas.

"'Course, the thing of it is, these locally owned stores are biting the dust," said Shirley Brock, who began work in the ladies' apparel department years ago. "A lot of times the heirs don't want to have anything to do with it and let it go."

That's not the case here. The store, opened in 1869 in Centerville with founder Col. H. M. Cook, who was a Confederate colonel. The store operation has since been passed down through seven generations, keeping the family business running for more than fourteen decades.

The square hole in the ceiling through which cashiers raised the money to the office on the second floor is still there. But the basket and that change-making system are long gone. "Oh yeah, we use computers," Brock said.

Upstairs in the store museum (no admission charge), you'll see a bunch of old ledgers, typewriters, store tokens, and an ad from a 1923 edition of the *Belton Journal* for the store's Dollar Day Specials—eight towels for a buck, eight bath rugs for a buck.

The oldest department store in Texas PARIS PERMENTER AND JOHN BIGLEY

The store puts out a brochure that outlines its history and lists employees by name, position, and how long they've worked there. Elsie York worked at the store as a bookkeeper from 1937 until 2008.

Ready, Set, Blow!
Burton

At the annual Burton Cotton Gin Festival, contestants—there are divisions for both kids and adults—line up on a stage set up under a big tent, waiting to compete in the bubble gum blowing contest. Officials distribute the gum, allowing contestants to work it over in their mouths. Then it's "On your mark, get set, blow bubbles!"

Whoever blows the biggest bubble wins. At this contest a panel of grandmotherly ladies sitting in lawn chairs with their feet up on hay bales do the judging.

"Come on, Justin—blow!" a woman in the crowd screamed at a little boy who was competing in the twelve-and-under division.

The Burton Cotton Gin is the official cotton gin of Texas.
PARIS PERMENTER AND JOHN BIGLEY

The festival is held in the spring to raise money for the maintenance and preservation of the town's circa 1914 cotton gin at the Texas Cotton Gin Museum (cottonginmuseum.org; 307 N. Main, 979-289-3378). Tours are available daily. Group tours are available with twenty-four hours' notice.

World's Largest Squirrel
Cedar Creek

At over fourteen feet tall, Ms. Pearl isn't just a Texas-sized squirrel but, according to Berdoll Pecan Candy and Gift Company (berdollpecanfarm .com; 2626 TX 71 West, 800-518-3870), she's the world's largest squirrel. Folks don't just brake for the pecan pralines and pecan pies (sold out of a

Even big dogs won't try to chase down Ms. Pearl. PARIS PERMENTER AND JOHN BIGLEY

vending machine in front of the Berdoll store for after-hours travelers), but also to get their photo taken with Ms. Pearl.

Standing sentry (and holding a pecan in her hands, naturally), Ms. Pearl has greeted travelers at the store since 2011, standing patiently for photos with as many as 100 people per day.

Ms. Pearl even has her own website, filled with photos by happy travelers: berdollsquirrel.com.

The Dime Box
Dime Box

There's not a lot to do in the village of Dime Box, but with a name like that, it's a fun detour for travelers. The burg is located just east of TX 21 on FM 141.

The town was originally known as Brown's Mill for its sawmill but confusion with towns with similar names led to its name change. The reason for the unusual moniker? Early residents could drop their mail—and a dime—in a box at the post office for delivery.

Today a transparent box housing an oversized Liberty Head dime is a fun photo stop in this dime-sized town that got national attention in 1945 when it was the country's first community to have 100 percent participation in the new March of Dimes campaign. Dime Box's citizens filled a mailbox with their collected donations and sent the package—mailbox and all—to President Franklin D. Roosevelt, who responded with a call to the city's postmaster.

Buddy can you spare a dime?
PARIS PERMENTER AND JOHN BIGLEY

Judge Williamson's statue on the courthouse square in Georgetown, the county seat of Williamson County. PARIS PERMENTER AND JOHN BIGLEY

Three-Legged Willie
Georgetown

The county seat of Williamson County is home of the statue of Three-Legged Willie, the moniker for Judge Robert McAlpin Williamson. The justice on the Republic of Texas Supreme Court suffered from tubular arthritis as a boy, causing his right leg to bend at a 90–degree angle. To compensate for his bent leg, Williamson wore a wooden leg from the knee down—giving him the appearance of having three legs.

Today the statue of Williamson can be seen in front of The Williamson Museum on the Georgetown Square (williamsonmuseum.org; 716 S. Austin Ave., 512-943-1670).

Billy the Kid
Hico

Hico is ate up with Billy the Kid. Billy the Kid Day is held the first weekend in April, with mock gunfights, people dressed in Western clothing, and

Could this be Billy the Kid? PARIS PERMENTER AND JOHN BIGLEY

sometimes a cattle drive through town. A statue downtown shows Billy the Kid drawing down on somebody with a gun. There's a small Billy the Kid Museum that carries Billy the Kid T-shirts.

Why all the fuss about Billy the Kid? Well, for one thing, it brings tourists to Hico (pronounced "hike-o"). So to keep the visitors coming, the town promotes the legend that Billy died here. Green markers around town recount the story. Without Billy, there wouldn't be much reason to come to Hico.

"I guess Billy and our historical buildings are our only real tourist attractions," said Bob Hefner, who started up the Billy the Kid Museum (billythe kidmuseum.com; 114 N. Pecan St., 254-796-2523), in 1987. "So for our economy, he's been very good to us."

Widely accepted history says Billy the Kid was shot dead at the age of twenty-one by Sheriff Pat Garrett in July 1881 at Fort Sumner, New Mexico. Hefner says different. Hefner contends Billy the Kid was really Brushy Bill Roberts, who keeled over of a heart attack on the sidewalk at the age of ninety on December 27, 1950, across the street from what is now the Rutledge-Jones Funeral Home.

So do people here really believe Brushy Bill Roberts was Billy the Kid, who had come to Hico to live out his final days? Hefner sure does.

"We can prove real easy Garrett didn't kill him," Hefner said. He said he's done research that shows a warrant went out for Billy the Kid's arrest the year after he was supposedly killed.

The Hutto Hippos
Hutto

Hutto is obsessed with hippos, not the real sort but the statuary kind. First, you've got a 14,900-pound concrete hippo on East Street named Henrietta that cost $2,000. Then there's Howdy, an eighteen-inch-high concrete hippo weighing 250 pounds that was purchased for $130 and introduced at the town's Hippo Festival in 2002.

Another herd of hippos hit Hutto (tourtexas.com/destinations/Hutto) in the spring of 2003 when Hutto was officially declared the "Hippo Capital of Texas." Local businesses ponied up $5,300 for fifty-four concrete hippos that weigh anywhere from 30 to 725 pounds. The squatting, smiling statues can be seen all around Hutto, in front of schools, homes, and businesses.

But the most grandiose of the town's hippo plans never happened. Hutto's Hippo Project Group had planned to build a $75,000 hippo named Hugo, which would have been thirty feet tall if you counted the ten-foot base. The hippo would have been the largest in the world, according to Hutto's former mayor Mike Fowler.

But the suggestion to build the big hippo with sales tax money set off a couple of the town's City Council members, who didn't think using public funds would be appropriate for putting up a fifteen-foot-wide, forty-foot-long, twenty-foot-tall, fiberglass-and-steel hippo, possibly on school property, with its own lighting, landscaping, and security measures.

So Hugo never appeared.

But that did not deter Fowler, who kept seeing hippos on Hutto's horizon.

"Hugo never happened, but we did deliver a life-size fiberglass hippo to the high school," he said. "We're just glad to have one there."

Legend has it this all started in 1915, when a hippo escaped from a circus train in Hutto and was later found wallowing in mud in Cottonwood Creek, from which the rotund beast was extricated with considerable hubbub. Soon

Hutto's high school is the only school in the country with a hippo mascot.

PARIS PERMENTER AND JOHN BIGLEY

after the incident—the most excitement the town had ever seen—the school adopted the hippopotamus as their mascot.

Hutto got into the hippo statue game when the chamber of commerce put up Henrietta—providing a photo opportunity for townspeople and tourists, since she's equipped with a set of stairs so kids can climb up and sit on her. Henrietta has her own "HIPPO XING" sign, and she's so popular that people keep stealing her ears.

Fowler is nuts about the hippo concept. When it was suggested to him that Hutto might put so-called Hippo Humps—speed bumps that would look like the tops of hippo heads with big eyes—in its streets, he said he liked the idea. "Anything that enhances the hippo is something that would be very unique to this community," he said.

Jailhouse Ghosts
La Grange

What was the first thing that the La Grange Area Chamber of Commerce (lagrangetx.org) used to talk about with new hires on their first day at work? According to Cathy Chaloupka, the chamber's former tourism director, one of those initial conversations was "Let's talk about the ghosts."

Until recently, the chamber had its offices at 171 South Main St., in the gothic stone building that used to be the Fayette County Jail. The spooky building, built in 1883, was used as a jail until 1985. When the chamber moved in, it was one ghostly incident after the next, Chaloupka said.

The upstairs room where the "Widow Dach" starved herself to death has seen a lot of action. Ironically, this former cell is the room where the chamber kept a refrigerator. Mrs. Dach was imprisoned in the late 1920s or early 1930s for killing her hired hand, said former chamber president Margo Johnson.

Nobody wanted to be in the Widow Dach room when the sun went down. "Anybody who ever officed here has refused to be here after dark," Johnson explained. "They just feel something. Like somebody's watching them."

"One night, when I was here by myself, I heard this horrible crash," Johnson said. She looked around and discovered that a large painting that had been hanging on a wall in the big room had been moved to the floor.

"So, if that's where they wanted it, that's where we left it," said the former chamber president.

Anyway, Chaloupka said one morning around 6:30, she was putting something in the refrigerator when she looked over at the steel jailhouse door that is the entryway to the Widow Dach's room. "There was an apparition as tall as the doorway, and I had a tingling feeling on my neck, like I was being watched," Chaloupka said.

Maybe the Widow Dach was looking for the mustard.

On another day, the former tourism director was in the big, high-ceilinged room on the ground floor. "I heard the sound of enormous chains dropping," she said. "I got up and looked around, and there was nothing there. It was like a hoist you would use to lift motors. A very heavy sound."

Drawers would slam. Footsteps were heard. Paintings got moved. Once a lightbulb flew out of a light fixture and landed in front of Chaloupka.

And it just kept getting weirder and weirder.

In September of 2005, a hangman's rope that dangled from the ceiling on the first floor started swaying back and forth on its own. "It just started

Do you believe in ghosts? PARIS PERMENTER AND JOHN BIGLEY

swinging like someone threw it, and no one was near the rope," said Rachel Bolfik, who was the chamber's member services director at the time. "There was nobody back there except these two ladies who were about twenty feet away from it."

So what'd they do? "Started cryin'," Bolfik recalled. "Ran out of the room, 'cause it just freaked 'em out."

Since the chamber moved to new offices elsewhere, the Old Jail has become a local history museum. You can come do your own ghost hunting during the museum's free, public visiting hours Monday through Friday from 8 a.m. to 5 p.m.

Capitol Expenditure

Is it any wonder that Texans love beef? Hey, if it weren't for cattle, Texas wouldn't have the lovely capitol building it has today.

In 1882, Texas needed a new capitol, but it was short of money to build one. One thing the state had plenty of, however, was unsettled ranch land just fit for a herd. Boy, did they have land. So the state legislature traded three million acres of public domain in the Panhandle in exchange for the construction of a capitol. A Chicago syndicate obtained the contract. When the capitol was completed in 1888, the value of the trade was calculated at about $1 per acre. The land later became the famed XIT Ranch.

Texas Hatters
Lockhart

The late Manny Gammage knew how to make a custom Western hat any way you wanted it. He could even make a hat that could cause fistfights, according to his daughter, Joella Gammage Torres, who runs Texas Hatters (texashatters.com; 911 S. Commerce St., 512-398-4287 or toll free 800-421-4287).

As a youngster in Houston, Manny made an unusual cowboy hat with a felt brim and straw crown. (These days, the hat is made by Texas Hatters and sold under the name of the "Half-Breed.") He'd wear it to the rodeo to see what kind of trouble it would get him into. More often than not, the hat caused a stir. So Manny knew what to do when he got the following letter:

"Dear Manny," the letter began, "I'm a big, ugly tattooed sumbitch with twenty-six years in the Army and I'm queer for hats. I want a hat for me that will scare women and children and start fights in Wyoming bars."

Manny didn't duplicate the felt and straw model for the letter writer. Instead, he came up with another model that would do the trick. Joella said her daddy made the customer a brown derby decorated with big silver conchos. There's no word on whether the man ever wore his derby in a Wyoming saloon or elementary school to test it out. But he was satisfied with the finished product.

"He sent a picture of himself in it and said it was a perfect choice," Joella said.

The store has also made hats to order for President Reagan and the two George Bushes, as well as Willie Nelson. Not everyone who buys a Texas Hatters hat wants to go a couple of rounds.

Oil patch art at its finest. PARIS PERMENTER AND JOHN BIGLEY

Whimsical Pump Jacks
Luling

With nearly 200 petroleum pump jacks in the city limits, Luling has painted and decorated many of these pump jacks as everything from football players to butterflies to watermelon slices. They make good photo stops. The Luling Chamber of Commerce provides a Pump Jack Tour map to all of the sites.

Luling Watermelon Thump
Luling

So how do you spit a watermelon seed 68 feet and 9 1/8 inches? Practice, practice, practice.

"I grew up in East Texas back in the 1950s, and we lived in the oil patch," said Lee Wheelis, who set the former *Guinness* world record for watermelon

The world's largest watermelon. PARIS PERMENTER AND JOHN BIGLEY

seed spitting at this festival in 1989. "And about the only entertainment we had was throwing watermelon rinds at each other and spitting seeds at each other. So it kind of comes natural."

Wheelis, who lives in Luling and retired from the Exxon Pipeline Company, described his technique this way: "You just kind of roll your tongue around it and give it a heave." Wheelis said he didn't know at first that he'd had a good spit when he set the record, which has since been beaten. "I didn't realize it 'cause there was a lot of people standing around, so I couldn't see where it landed," he recalled. "But when everybody went to hollering and screaming, well, then, I knew what had happened."

The annual Luling Watermelon Thump is held the last full weekend in June. In 1999, the town painted a new water tower to look like a watermelon.

If you're ready to go the spittin' distance, call (830) 875-3214, ext. 303, or check out watermelonthump.com.

Keep an eye out for the Hairy Man! PARIS PERMENTER AND JOHN BIGLEY

Hairy Man Road
Round Rock

The Pacific Northwest has its Sasquatch. Mexico and South Texas have the Chupacabra. And Central Texas has the Hairy Man.

The legend of Round Rock's Hairy Man dates to pioneer days. Various versions of the local legend say a young boy either fell off a wagon as pioneers headed west or was separated from his family by flood waters. Then the boy either lived alone in the woods or was raised by local animals. Eventually the boy grew into a man and became a hermit and, well, very hairy. I guess this guy must have looked like the caveman in those old Geico TV commercials.

The story says the hairy man frequently tried to chase away strangers and would hide in the trees to scare passers-by, sometimes sitting up in the tree canopy which grew over the road, dragging his feet on the top of passing stagecoaches. One day, he supposedly fell in front of a stagecoach and was trampled to death, doomed to haunt the shady road to this day.

Round Rock celebrates this unusual legend with the annual Hairy Man Festival. Held in October to tie in with Halloween, the festival features the usual festival fare—crafts, food, music, kids' activities—and some not so usual festival fun as well. The most unusual festival activity is the Hairy Man Contest, judging, yes, the hairiest contestant.

Try your luck spotting the Hairy Man on Hairy Man Road, found west of Round Rock, just off Sam Bass Road.

If You've Got the Nuts, They've Got the Crackers
Seguin

Looking for some real nuts? If that's your story, then visit this town, where you will find what was once billed as the World's Largest Pecan, a one-thousand-pound concrete nut statue on the Guadalupe County Courthouse Square.

This is also the home of Pape's Pecan House (papepecan.com; 101 S. Hwy. 123 Bypass, 830-379-7442), a retail pecan shop and the home of owner Kenneth Pape's massive collection of nutcrackers. For decades, Pape, a pecan grower by trade, has been collecting both decorative and functional crackers of nuts.

"I've got about six thousand nutcrackers," said Pape, who picks up nutcrackers while traveling all over the world, from antiques shops, and eBay.

With all those nutcrackers around, it's a good thing Pape likes eating nuts and not just cracking them open.

"I guess I make my living out of 'em, so I enjoy them," he said. "They're real healthy. I eat quite a few."

You got Bugs Bunny nutcrackers, Mickey Mouse nutcrackers, Easter Bunny nutcrackers, dog nutcrackers, squirrel nutcrackers, alligator nutcrackers, a nutcracker that looks like Charles de Gaulle, an Aunt Jemima nutcracker, a Popeye nutcracker, and nutcracker soldiers with fuzzy hats that serve as barstools. You just sit on the hat. Some of the nutcrackers are even a bit risqué.

Nutcrackers have been around as long as there have been nuts that needed cracking. The British, Pape said, have been into cracking their nuts since at least the Elizabethan period. "They used to take them to the theaters to watch Shakespeare," Pape said. "They'd crack their filberts and throw them on the floor, just like we would peanuts."

You kinda get the idea of what you're getting into here when you see the large likeness of a squirrel carrying a big nut like a football on the wall out in front of the store. There are even machines that crack nuts among Pape's collection.

No longer just the world's largest, today Seguin's is the world's oldest, largest pecan. PARIS PERMENTER AND JOHN BIGLEY

Archives War

It would be interesting to speculate what would have happened to the city of Austin if Sam Houston had gotten away with his attempt to steal the republic's records out of Austin and move the capital back to Houston. Would it mean that Austin wouldn't have developed into the hippie-dippy city it is today? Would there be no piercing parlors on Sixth Street, the city's music and nightlife area? Would there be no garage bands in the Live Music Capital of the World? Would the University of Texas be in River Oaks, that tony Houston development, instead of in Austin?

In December 1842, Sam Houston, president of Texas, ordered Texas's official records removed from the Land Office in Austin and taken to Houston to reestablish that city as the capital. (Houston had been named the capital in 1837. In 1839, when Mirabeau B. Lamar was president, he moved the capital to Waterloo, a small settlement that later became Austin.)

Houston wanted the capital back in Houston, his namesake. So he dispatched three wagons and about twenty men to sneak the records back to Houston. This was kind of like when the Baltimore Colts took off in the middle of the night and moved to Indianapolis. Except this time, it didn't work. An armed posse of Austinites cut the paperwork thieves off at the pass and took back the records. So the state records stayed in Austin. The so-called Archives War was over, and Austin remains to this day the capital of the Lone Star State.

I bet a lot of conservative state legislators probably wish Houston had been successful in his attempt to get the capital out of the liberal enclave.

"This is real rare," said Pape, showing off a power-driven pecan-cracking device made in 1926 in San Antonio. "It was called a Jim Dandy pecan cracker. It's an electric motor. It crushes the nuts and drops them into a box down below." An illustration on a pane of glass at the top of the machine shows two cartoon elves smashing their nuts with sledgehammers, while a third elf is carrying around one of his big nuts in a wheelbarrow.

Pape is so nuts about nuts that he's even constructed a pecan on wheels—yes, it's the World's Largest Mobile Pecan. The sixteen-foot-long creation (which replaced a 2002 pecan of Pape's that had won and then lost the world's record) makes its appearance in parades and special events.

Willie's Golf Course
Spicewood

When you're a Texas icon and you own your own golf course, you can make up whatever goofy rules you want. That explains why Willie Nelson's Pedernales Country Club Cut 'N Putt—the only country club I've ever seen with a trough urinal in the men's room—lists some unusual rules for golfers on its website, including:

- When another player is shooting, no player should talk, whistle, hum, clink coins, or pass gas.
- Excessive displays of affection are discouraged. Violators must replace divots and will be penalized five strokes.
- Replace divots, smooth footprints in bunkers, brush backtrail with branches, park car under brush, and have the office tell your spouse you're in a conference.

It's Willie's Place PARIS PERMENTER AND JOHN BIGLEY

- No more than twelve in your foursome.
- Gambling is forbidden of course, unless you're stuck or you need a legal deduction for charitable or educational expenses.
- No bikinis, mini-skirts, skimpy see-through, or sexually exploitative attire allowed. Except on women.

Perhaps the most remarkable aspect of the course is that you never know who you'll run into. On an October day in 2005, Texas gubernatorial candidate and writer Kinky Friedman was holding a campaign fundraiser that was attended by Jesse Ventura, former wrestler and former governor of Minnesota.

While schmoozing, Ventura, who was sporting two three-inch-long beard pigtails that flapped rhythmically when he spoke, addressed a variety of unrelated subjects—the Kennedy assassination (it's a conspiracy, he claimed), how he had recently caught a large fish off his dock, how you can trust people with tattoos because they're not putting on airs, and those annoying people who shake your hand too hard.

"I don't like squeezers," Ventura explained. "Everybody thinks 'cause you got muscles they got to squeeze you. That's nonsense." Of course, when you're as large as Ventura is, you can say whatever you want to and nobody will tell you to shut up.

Meanwhile, people were waiting for Willie to arrive so that the Friedman supporters who had paid $5,000 a head to play with Willie could get started. Various tournament officials roamed the parking lot with cell phones to their ears, trying to track down Willie, who eventually showed.

None of this seemed to bother Friedman, who apparently had no intention of playing at his own fundraiser. "I find golf stultifyingly dull," he said. "The only two good balls I ever hit was when I stepped on the garden rake."

For more inspiring information, go to cutnputt.com.

Dr Pepper Museum
Waco

Everything you ever wanted to know about Dr Pepper can be answered here. Almost.

"There are twenty-three flavors in the drink, but we—the staff—don't know what they are," said Judy Shofner, the museum's former archivist. "But it doesn't have prune juice. Everybody thinks it has prune juice. It has a very strong apricot base, which people may be mistaking for prune juice."

Listen to the talking animatron of Dr. Charles Alderton, who concocted Dr Pepper in 1885 while working as a pharmacist at the nearby Old Corner

Don't be afraid of the Dr. PARIS PERMENTER AND JOHN BIGLEY

Drug Store. At first, the drink had a different name. "In those days they called it a Waco," the animatron dressed in a charcoal suit tells visitors.

The museum (drpeppermuseum.com; 300 S. 5th St., 254-757-1025) has a collection of the various bottles Dr Pepper has used over the years, a bottle-cleaning machine, a soda fountain where you can get an old-fashioned soda fountain–style Dr Pepper, and a gift shop with Dr Pepper hat pins, mouse pads, coin purses, and refrigerator magnets.

Buffalo Hair Ball
Waco

"There seems to be more interest in that darned old hair ball than there is in the museum," stewed Stew Lauterbach, former curator of the Texas Ranger Hall of Fame and Museum (texasranger.org; 100 Texas Ranger Tr., 254-750-8631), a tribute to the elite law enforcement unit formed in 1823 to protect Stephen F. Austin's colony from the Comanches.

The museum is far more than a hair ball. PARIS PERMENTER AND JOHN BIGLEY

That explains why museum officials took what was billed as a buffalo hair ball off display and put it in storage in a vault. You could say the hair ball has been mothballed.

"Unfortunately, it is what we are known for," said Christina Stopka, deputy director of Operations and director of the Texas Ranger Research Center. "It almost looks like a cannonball, is what it looks like. It's not."

Lauterbach said the other problem with the item is that the museum couldn't identify it as a bona fide, genuine buffalo hair ball. "So we don't want to perpetuate a myth we're not able to substantiate, one way or another," he explained.

Au contraire, said Tom Burks, former curator of the museum. He said the item is an actual buffalo hair ball, once owned by the late Gaines de Graffenreid, another of the museum's former curators.

"Yeah, he was very pleased with it," Burks said. "He thought it was a museum item. And the odd, funny thing about it was people would come in the museum and spot that. And they'd go all over the museum to come see that, more than they would Santa Anna's sword."

The Health Camp
Waco

The most inappropriately named restaurant in Texas, this greasy burger joint at 2601 Circle Road (health-camp-waco.com; 254-752-2186), on "the Circle" (one of Texas's few remaining traffic circles), sells an item called a Super Health Burger. That's a double-decker bun with two meat patties, lettuce and tomato, two slices of Old English cheese, and "special dressing." Perhaps the closest thing on the menu to health food is the onion rings.

So, how did the Health Camp, which opened in 1949, get the aerobics class–sounding name?

"It's a real strange story," said June Smith, the former manager. The name came about when Jack Schaevetz, the original owner, was trying to

Which way to the workout room? PARIS PERMENTER AND JOHN BIGLEY

come up with something to call the place. All he could think of, she said, were the words "Health Camp," which were stamped on top of each egg his mother bought from the farmer down the road, when Jack was a little boy.

So why were the words "Health Camp" stamped on the eggs? "He had no earthly idea," June said.

The place also sells steak fingers, which begs the question: How can there be steak fingers if cows ain't got no hands?

The Zorn Bowling Club
Zorn

When the bartender here told me that the annual dues at this private nine-pins bowling club on TX 123 (zornbowling.samsbiz.com; 830-379-5247) were "five thirty five" a year, I thought she meant $535.

Actually, it was only $5.35 a year—although these days it's shot up a few bits. And it's a few extra bucks for club members to bowl. But it sure ain't no $535 a year membership fee.

The bowling alley is about as unautomated as a bowling alley can get and still have electric lighting. They use human pinsetters. Mostly, the children of its members set the pins on the four lanes in the club. The pinsetters sit on a perch between lanes behind the pins. As you look down the lanes, you can see their legs hanging down.

The Zorn Bowling Club has been in operation since 1912. Clayton Roberson, a member of the club's board of directors, said today the club probably has 180 to 200 members.

The ninepin game they play is a little different from regular tenpin. Teams of six bowlers square off. Instead of being lined up in a triangle, the pins are in a diamond shape. Each bowler rolls two balls. The next bowler up has to deal with whatever the previous bowler has left standing. But the team captain sets the order of who bowls when. So he gets to pick which bowler on the team should bowl in particular situations.

Knocking down all nine pins is called a "ringer." A ringer scores nine points. But the ideal thing to do is to leave the pin in the middle of the diamond standing. If you can pull that off, you get twelve points.

There's one significant similarity between tenpin and ninepin. You can drink beer while playing either one.

Hill Country

The scenic beauty of the Texas Hill Country is legendary, a land of sparkling rivers and streams, dramatic canyons, glorious spring wildflowers, ancient live oaks, and pastoral villages.

Sitting on the Edwards Plateau, the terrain contains natural wonders like Enchanted Rock State Natural Area, an enormous pink granite dome rising 425 feet above ground, the second largest in the country. Dozens of state parks and state natural areas offer fishing, tubing, kayaking, hiking, and biking. The rugged limestone hills conceal seven stunning show caves.

Lush green valleys and rolling hills encompass enchanting little towns, like Wimberley and Marble Falls, with endless gift shops, upscale boutiques, artisans' studios, and tearooms.

Fredericksburg, with its rich German heritage, offers Biergartens and tasty wursts. Its main street, lined with one-of-a-kind shops and eateries, attracts visitors year-round. In addition, dozens of fine vineyards and wineries nestle in the countryside around Fredericksburg.

The first letters of the ten streets east of Fredericksurg's Gillespie County courthouse spell "all welcome", and the first letters of the eight streets west of the courthouse invite you to come back.

Known for the many dude ranches that surround it, Bandera, "Cowboy Capital of the World," is the land of cowboys, rodeos, dance halls, honkytonks, and Lone Star beer. The town looks like a movie set right out of an old Western flick, complete with horses on Main Street.

Kinky Friedman, singer, songwriter, satirist, humorist, author, and 2006 gubernatorial candidate, is perhaps one of the most colorful characters living in the Hill Country. Actually, the hills are full of entertaining "good ol' boys" and curious folks with fascinating hobbies.

Shoppers will think they've found paradise with all the antiques shops, and foodies will find a dozen mouth-watering BBQ joints vying for the title of best in the state.

It's said that no one can visit the Hill Country only once.

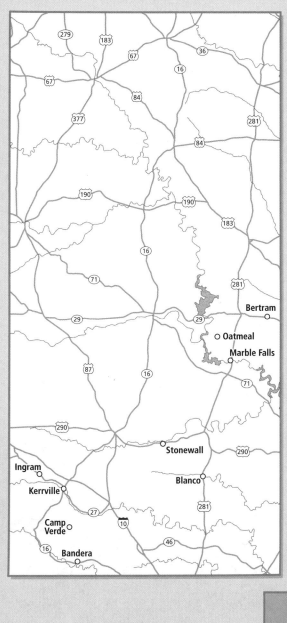

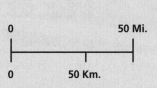

0   50 Mi.

0   50 Km.

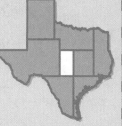

Hill Country

Check Out the Shrunken Head on That Chick
Bandera

One reason you won't want to miss the Frontier Times Museum (frontier timesmuseum.org; 510 13th St., 830-796-3864) is that the shrunken head has been returned.

The tiny head of a seventeen-year-old Ecuadoran Indian woman went on a road trip back in 2002, when somebody stole the head from the museum, then threw it on the side of the road in San Antonio. Maybe the thief or thieves couldn't get much for the head at a pawn shop. Maybe the pawn shop owner was looking for a larger head. Anyway, after the head was found by a construction worker, police returned it to the museum.

And she's not going away again any time soon. "Now she's nailed to the counter," said Jane Graham, the museum's Docent Emeritus. You gotta do what you gotta do.

Speaking of heads, another of the museum's highlights is the two-headed goat, displayed in a glass case like the shrunken head.

A little bit of everything can be found here. PARIS PERMENTER AND JOHN BIGLEY

No small-town Texas museum would be complete without a stuffed version of the small Texas state mammal. "It's amazing how many people come from out of state and want to see an armadillo," Graham explained.

Mary Warren, a tourist from Ohio who was visiting the museum, immediately proved Graham's point. "We went to Enchanted Rock and saw one dead along the highway," she said.

Journalist J. Marvin Hunter built the museum in the 1930s to house his Western collection. Since then the collection has gone way beyond Western. Among the items you'll see here are one of those Murphy beds that used to fold up into the wall, a Lone Ranger snow globe, an 1848 Mexican bed roll, a corn planter, an ancient hair curler that looks like a torture device with electrical cords and clips hanging down, and the skull of an Incan woman.

How did the museum come by the skull? "I was told someone in their RV was driving through and they said, 'Will you take it?'" Graham said.

So Many Movie Cowboys, So Little Time
Bandera

If you don't like looking at John Wayne, stay out of the Old Spanish Trail Restaurant at 305 Main St. (830-796-3836).

The walls of the back dining room are lined with hundreds of paintings and photos of America's favorite red-blooded Western guy. You've got John Wayne in an Army uniform from *The Green Berets* (even though he never served in the military), John Wayne as Davy Crockett in a coonskin cap from *The Alamo*, and John Wayne in matching high heels and bag. We just made that last part up.

"He's just always been like a hero of mine, and I always thought that Bandera was perfect for that room," said Gwen Janes, who has owned the restaurant since 1978.

People donate to the collection. Janes said a huge canvas of Wayne was donated to her by a guy in Florida because his wife hated it. "She said, 'Get that thing out of my living room,'" Janes said. "Mamma said it had to go."

Mamma sounds more like John Wayne than John Wayne does.

It should come as no surprise that Janes's ex-husband, Rudy Robbins, was one of John Wayne's stuntmen. "We're no longer married, but he lives here in Bandera," Janes said.

Conversely, John Wayne never made it into Janes's restaurant. She said customers tell her she ought to tell people that he ate here. "I say, 'No, I'm

Slow down there, Pilgrim, and mosey over to the OST.
PARIS PERMENTER AND JOHN BIGLEY

not going to lie to them about it'," Janes said. John Wayne wouldn't have lied about it, either.

If you don't get enough of John Wayne from the wall hangings, they keep a DVD player in the John Wayne room and play John Wayne movies.

Dinosaur Made from Auto, Truck, and Other Junked Parts
Bertram

The head is two oil pans rigged up to a windshield-wiper motor. Turn it on and the dinosaur's jaw flaps. "The teeth are spark plugs," said the late Garrett Wilkinson, the artist who welded it. "It has one-hundred-four spark plugs, if that means anything." The toes are off a farm cultivator. "And those vertebrae welded in the neck—those are the rocker arms for your valves," he explained.

The Bertram dinosaur is named Lizzie. PARIS PERMENTER AND JOHN BIGLEY

Wilkinson built two junk dinosaurs in his lifetime. He built the first one after Bertram city officials asked him to make a beast to go along with the discovery of some dinosaur tracks in the creek at nearby Oatmeal.

"The city asked me if I would build 'em a dinosaur to bring in tourists," Wilkinson said. "I told 'em, 'Well, I don't know how I'd make the skin on it.' But I told 'em I could make the skeleton."

The second dinosaur was built because of popular demand, after he sold the first one to a man from San Angelo. "When I sold it, people would drive by and say, 'Where's that dinosaur? I drove all the way from Houston to see that dinosaur.' So I decided I needed to build another dinosaur."

The second dinosaur, Lizzie, is popular in parades. It can still be seen in Bertram, parked on TX 29 as you come into town from the east, or outside Wilkinson's old welding shop on Vaughan Street Though there's no official address, 523 E. State Hwy 29 should get you in sight of it.

"At Christmastime we put lights on him and plug him in and light him up," said Shirlene Vaughn, Wilkinson's daughter.

Though he passed away in 1999, Wilkinson created over one hundred whimsical metal folk sculptures during his lifetime, many of which can be seen around Bertram.

An Appetite for Bowling
Blanco

The decor in the big dining room features bowling balls, bowling trophies, bowling bags, and bowling lockers. It's not your average dining setting, but you are eating at the Blanco Bowling Club Cafe (blancobowlingclub.com; 310 4th St., 830-833-4416), a place that comes with a half dozen ninepin bowling lanes. More than 200 people belong to the private bowling club. The cafe, open to the public, is a big hit around town and in the Hill Country.

"A lot of 'em like the enchiladas," said John L. Dechert, president of the bowling club. "A lot of 'em like the chicken-fried steak. The hamburgers are awful good." And the lemon and coconut meringue pies in the case behind the counter are probably six inches tall.

On one Sunday morning the place was abuzz with people who all seemed to know one another and were checking one another out to make sure they'd been to church that morning. "What are you doin' in here? You must be lost," said an old boy in a pair of suspenders to some old gal. "Well, I go to church over here," she answered.

John is proud of the cafe's plastic sign out front that shows a brightly colored illustration of a cheeseburger. "That was a real good investment,"

Only at the Blanco Bowling Club Cafe can you eat in a dining room decorated with bowling bags. PARIS PERMENTER AND JOHN BIGLEY

said John, who was wearing a George Strait baseball cap. "When it's lit up at night, you can see it from the main road. We're sort of off the beaten track. A lot of our business is word of mouth."

They nearly give the food away. Daily specials come in small, medium, or large portions, all reasonably priced. One reason the club can offer such low prices is that the building is paid for. The club bought the place in 1967 and made the last payment in 2003.

There are no automatic pinsetters. The local high school kids take care of that. "It's a pretty good job," John said. "For three hours of work they get pay, plus tips. And a lot of times the tip is as much as what they get paid." It's certainly enough to gain ten or twenty pounds eating in here.

It's a Bird, It's a Plane, It's a Camel
Camp Verde

Camp Verde, the Army post on the banks of Verde Creek, is probably most famous for the great "camel experiment." In 1854, U.S. Secretary of War Jefferson Davis had a bright idea to use camels for supply transport in the dry Southwest. Congress appropriated the money, and the first shipment of thirty-three camels and four drivers arrived from Egypt in 1856.

This sign is a reminder of the past at Camp Verde. PARIS PERMENTER AND JOHN BIGLEY

Who's Who

If you ain't from Texas, you ain't . . . oh, never mind. Let's not repeat that oft-seen bumper sticker cliché. On the other hand, it is true that an inordinate number of famous people are or were from Texas. Let's drop a few names here, without even mentioning Willie: Beyoncé, Selena Gomez, Jessica Simpson, Matthew McConaughey, Jim Parsons, Kelly Clarkson, Renée Zellweger, Jared Padalecki, Jensen Ackles, Owen and Luke Wilson, Miranda Lambert, Jamie Foxx, Eva Longoria, George Foreman, sausage dude and singer Jimmy Dean, football star Earl Campbell, Waylon Jennings, Tommy Lee Jones, pianist Van Cliburn, race car driver A. J. Foyt, Sissy Spacek, Kenny Rogers, Dennis and Randy Quaid, Rip Torn, Sam Donaldson, Dan Rather, Bob Schieffer, Linda Ellerbee, columnist Liz Smith, Walter Cronkite, brother actors Dana Andrews and Steve Forrest, dancer Tommy Tune, movie critic Rex Reed, TV animator Mike Judge (*Beavis and Butthead*), Mike Nesmith of the Monkees, Freddie Fender, Lyle Lovett, George Strait, Joan Crawford, Janis Joplin, Roy Orbison, Ben Crenshaw, Tom Kite, Babe Zaharias, George Jones, Barbara Mandrell, Dale Evans, Gene Autry, Lee Trevino, Lance Armstrong, Nolan Ryan, writer Dan Jenkins, Ben Hogan, baseball hall of famer Frank Robinson, Carl Lewis, and former Presidents Lyndon B. Johnson and George W. Bush.

During the Civil War, the camp was captured by Confederate forces; when the war ended and the fort was recaptured, there were more than one hundred camels. The experiment worked! The camels could carry heavier loads and travel longer distances than horses or mules, but the War Department ended the experiment and deactivated the fort in 1869.

There appear to be several versions of what happened next. Camels were sold to zoos and circuses, and men tried to use them to haul various items to various places. Stories that they were let loose, turned wild, and terrified area inhabitants are generally disbelieved.

All that remains today is the restored general store built in 1857 to provide the soldiers with supplies, mostly liquor. Today, it's an upscale gift shop and cafe featuring oodles of camel memorabilia. It even has its own restaurant, open from 11 a.m. to 3 p.m. (campverdegeneralstore.com; 285 Camp Verde Rd. E. 830-634-7722).

Stonehenge II
Ingram

It started out with one large stone. Tile contractor Doug Hill of Hunt was building a patio at the time. When the job was completed, he had one stone left over.

He asked his neighbor, Al Shepperd, if he wanted it. "He said, 'Let me put on my shoes. I'll show you where I want you to put it,'" Doug recalled. "We brought it over here and put it next to the road, and he said, 'I kinda like this rock.'"

The stone, about 5 feet, 8 inches wide, was placed in a big field owned by Al, across FM 1340 from Doug's house. Doug noticed Shepperd really admired the stone. "I'd see him driving by real slow, looking at his rock out there," Doug said. "I thought it was a little odd, but he was a little eccentric anyway."

As time went by, Al began mowing larger and larger circles around the stone. Then one day he showed up with an article about Stonehenge, the ancient druid monument in England, and told Doug, "I'd like you to build something behind that stone that looks something like this."

The end result was a 92-foot-diameter hollow plaster re-creation of Stonehenge, flanked by two Easter Island statues, one on each end of the field. Doug said it took him about four and a half months to build it, with the help of three laborers.

Stonehenge II is Ingram's top photo stop. PARIS PERMENTER AND JOHN BIGLEY

Hiccup Cure

The only Texas gubernatorial candidate in 2006 with an announced hiccup cure? How 'bout author and humorist Kinky Friedman?

Though not a Democrat, the Kinkster, who ran as an independent, says the solution is to throw money at it.

Friedman's hiccup remedy came to light during a morning visit to Conchita's Mexican Cafe, a small place in downtown Kerrville. While Friedman was in there, Danita Horner, a seventeen-year-old waitress, was having a real problem with hiccups. We're talking a major hiccup attack. You could tell where she was located in the restaurant by tracking the noise. *Hiccup*, she's in the kitchen. *Hiccup*, she's in the dining room. *Hiccup*, she's by the counter.

It didn't take long for the impulsive and inventive Friedman to step in and take action. "Come over here; I've got a cure for those hiccups," he said in a commanding voice.

Danita quickly stepped over to Friedman's table. Then Friedman pulled his wallet out of his pants pocket, took out six twenty-dollar bills, and fanned them out on the table like a hand of cards. "One more hiccup, and it's all yours," Friedman told the young waitress.

She stood there, blinking, trying to squeeze off another hiccup. She couldn't do it. The thought of a quick $120 had driven them right out of her.

Friedman said he's tried that trick a half dozen or so times, and it's always worked. He thinks he got the idea from an old Kerrville cowboy named Grady Tuck. Either way, Kinky said the size of the bribe you need to use to drive away the hiccups depends on the wealth of the hiccup sufferer. So for a rich guy, you might have to put up a set of keys to a Hummer.

First, five arches of three fake stones each went up in the center. "When that was done, Al came into some money from the sale of a condominium, so we started on the outside circle," Doug said.

So why did Al want this *objet d'art* put on his land? "I think what inspired him was the publicity," said Doug, who lived across the road from *Stonehenge II*.

Al, who has since passed away, requested that his ashes be sprinkled on the ground around *Stonehenge II*, and thus lives on as part of his beloved project.

Presidential Treatment

President Lyndon Baines Johnson had a wicked sense of humor. When people would visit his ranch in Stonewall, outside Johnson City, he loved to take them for a ride in his little blue '62 model Amphicar built in West Germany. Of course, he didn't tell them that the vehicle was amphibious.

As he hollered that the brakes had failed, he'd run the vehicle into the Pedernales River as a joke. The convertible is still on display in the carport at the ranch.

Running his funny little car into the water wasn't President Johnson's only quirk. The late George Christian, LBJ's press secretary from 1966 until 1969, said the president was a gregarious fellow who didn't like being alone and never quit working. So he'd keep talking to his staff "while he was shaving, while he was showering, while he was on the pot, or whatever," Christian said. "He just kept on going."

Christian recalls the time the former president accidentally drenched him with his Water Pik. "One time he was brushing his teeth, and I was standing in the doorway taking notes, and Larry Temple [the president's attorney] was standing right behind me," Christian said. "And he [LBJ] looked up at me while he was using that Water Pik and squirted me from head to toe with Lavoris. The president just kept going. And I spent the rest of the day smelling like mouthwash."

Like the Energizer Bunny, Johnson kept going and going and going. "It didn't bother me seeing him naked, which was often, or in his pajamas," Christian said.

Another thing Johnson would do, Christian said, was eat your food as a joke. "When he was on a diet, which was all the time, he'd reach over and steal your ice cream," Christian said. "He didn't ask you, he just did it. He'd sit there and stare at your dessert, and the next thing you know, here comes this big old hand stealing your dessert or your butter."

The Shepperd family sold the land in the summer of 2010, and the Hill Country Arts Foundation (hcaf.com; 830-367-5121) in nearby Ingram raised enough money to purchase the entire collection and move it to the foundation's property. The pieces were all numbered, dismantled, transported, and put back together so visitors can still visit the unique tourist attraction.

See the World

Want to see the world without buying a plane ticket? Visit:

Athens, Texas 75751

Canadian, Texas 79014

China, Texas 77613

Egypt, Texas 77436

Ireland, Texas 76528

Italy, Texas 76651

Turkey, Texas 79261

London, Texas 76854

New London, Texas 75682

Paris, Texas 75460

Palestine, Texas 75801

Or just travel around the country:

Boston, Texas 75570

Cleveland, Texas 77327

Colorado City, Texas 79512

Columbus, Texas 78934

Denver City, Texas 79323

Detroit, Texas 75436

Klondike, Texas 75448

Memphis, Texas 79245

Miami, Texas 79059

Nevada, Texas 75173

Pasadena, Texas 77506

Reno, Texas 75462

Santa Fe, Texas 77517

Tennessee Colony, Texas 75861

Or even the universe:

Earth, Texas 79031

Mars, Texas 75778

Venus, Texas 76084

Dead Man's Hole
Marble Falls

Not a cheery location, Dead Man's Hole, south of town off CR 401, is a 155-foot-deep natural hole into which murdered Union sympathizers were pitched back around the time of the Civil War and the Reconstruction period that followed.

Former State Senator Walter Richter of Austin said that Adolph Hoppe, his great-grandfather, was one of seventeen people killed and tossed into the hole. Richter was instrumental in getting a historical marker placed at the site.

James Oakley, a former Burnet County commissioner, said there used to be a tree limb hanging over the hole. Offending parties were hanged over the hole, then cut loose and dumped into it.

A grate has been put over the hole to keep people from falling in—or being thrown in. "There are people who would delight in using Dead Man's Hole for Dead Man's Hole purposes," Richter explained.

Anybody down there? PARIS PERMENTER AND JOHN BIGLEY

Oatmeal Festival
Oatmeal

There are several stories about how this small town (population: 20) got its peculiar name. Some say it was because of a German named Habermill who settled the place in the 1840s. One version has it that Habermill meant "oatmeal" in German, "but the Germans who speak German say it doesn't," said Carolyn Smith, the former city secretary in nearby Bertram.

Guess what's for breakfast? PARIS PERMENTER AND JOHN BIGLEY

Another version of the origin story has the Scotch-Irish settlers who came after Habermill not being able to pronounce the German name correctly. "Habermill" sounded like "oatmeal" when they tried to say it the way Habermill did.

Either way, each Labor Day Weekend there is an Oatmeal Festival. Oatmeal flakes are sprinkled out of small airplanes flying overhead, and there is an oatmeal bake-off. In the past the festival also featured an oatmeal sculpture contest.

Ever thought about dropping cooked oatmeal out of the plane?

"Plop, plop, plop. I don't know about that," said Polly Krenek, Oatmeal's former city secretary. "We'd have a lot of people [saying], 'Don't look up when the oatmeal plane's flying over. You'll get oatmeal in the face.'"

"We still have the wacky games," Krenek added. "The oatmeal stacking and oatmeal-eating contest and that sort of thing." Oatmeal stacking? "You just take the regular oatmeal boxes, and whoever can stack the most and the highest wins," she explained.

Oh, it's easy to tell when you've reached Oatmeal (RM 243, five-and-a-half miles south of Bertram). The unincorporated town's water tower is painted red and gold to look like a Three-Minute Oats box.

Feeling a little flaky? Call the city of Bertram (512) 355-2197 or visit oatmealfestival.org.

North Texas

North Texas is a hugely diverse region, containing one of the largest metropolitan areas of the Southwest, Dallas–Fort Worth, with a population of over seven million. On the other hand, it also contains acres of bucolic countryside where dinosaurs once roamed.

Both Dallas and Fort Worth showcase historic as well as ultra-modern architecture and offer countless attractions. As a fashion center, Dallas features upscale shopping centers and large malls. It's also home to a sophisticated urban art scene with the Morton H. Meyerson Symphony Center, Dallas Museum of Art, fine galleries, and distinctive eateries.

Fort Worth promotes itself as the city of "Cowboys and Culture." Get a taste of the cowboy life at the Stockyards National Historic District, buy authentic Stetsons or Leddy's custom-made boots, eat finger-lickin' good Texas BBQ, hear good ol' Western tunes at the White Elephant Saloon, and watch a real live cattle drive down Exchange Avenue. Come evening, head for Billy Bob's, the world's largest honky-tonk, or one of the many other music venues.

Some folks are surprised to learn that Fort Worth's cultural district is second to none, with some of the most acclaimed art museums in the country, an exceptional Museum of Science and History, the National Cowgirl Museum, and one of the top five zoos in the United States. Sundance Square, Fort Worth's revitalized downtown, is home to the state-of-the-art Bass Performance Hall, music venues, classy shops, theaters, and restaurants.

Another popular attraction is the Bureau of Engraving and Printing, the only place you can see paper money being made outside Washington, D.C.

In addition to the "Metroplex," North Texas is home to interesting small towns, numerous winding rivers, some great state parks, nature preserves, and lakes providing excellent water sports and recreational opportunities.

Big Tex—Ho, Ho, Ho!
Dallas

In case you're from another planet and don't know who Big Tex is, he's the fifty-five-foot-tall icon of the State Fair of Texas. He's a native Texan, so he's B-I-G. He wears a ninety-five-gallon hat and size ninety-six boots. His jeans are made from seventy-two yards of denim and weigh sixty-five pounds.

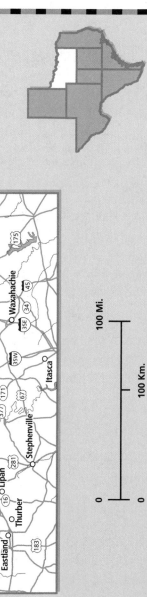

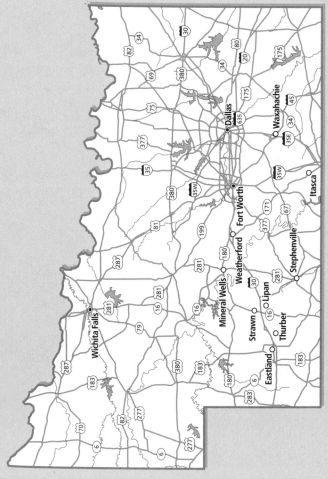

North Texas

100 Mi.

0

100 Km.

0

Texas State Symbols

Texans are so proud of their state that they have over forty-eight official state "this-es" and state "thats," including:

The armadillo is the official small state mammal.

The longhorn is the official large state mammal.

The horned toad is the official state reptile

The state musical instrument is the guitar, on which you can play…

The official state song, "Texas, Our Texas," although most people in the Lone Star State don't know the words to "Texas, Our Texas" and figure the state song is "The Eyes of Texas." But it's not, because that's a University of Texas song.

Chili is the official Texas state dish, although it probably ought to be actress Sandra Bullock, who has a house in Austin.

The state grass is sideoats grama, although in liberal Austin there are probably some hippies who think it oughta be wacky tabacky.

The state sport is rodeo, having apparently edged out the tractor pull.

The Mexican free-tailed bat is the official state flying mammal.

Want me to stop? Tough.

The lightning whelk is the official state seashell.

There are so many designated official state things in Texas that a move was afoot in 1997 to name an official state fungus. State Senator Chris Harris of Arlington filed a bill to name the devil's cigar fungus the official state fungus of Texas, because this fungus has been reported only in Texas and Japan. The bill made it through the state senate but, tragically, died in the house.

Big Tex's denim shirt is made by Ft. Worth's Dickies company.
KEVIN BROWN/STATE FAIR OF TEXAS

But not everyone knows he was born a Santa Claus! Constructed by the Kerens Chamber of Commerce from papier mâché and drill casings in 1949, his purpose was to boost holiday sales. Sold in 1951, Santa was transformed into a cowboy and made his debut at the 1952 state fair. He's presided over every state fair since then. The late radio announcer Jim Lowe holds the record for being the booming voice of Big Tex for thirty-nine years.

Over the years Big Tex has had various minor surgeries. Then, during the 2012 fair, Big Tex suffered third-degree burns when his electronics shorted out and caused a major fire. But you can't keep a Texas hero down! By the time the 2013 fair opened, Big Tex was back on the job with some spiffy new (fireproof) duds, booming his familiar welcome: "Howdy, folks!" Feeling larger than life? Go see Big Tex for yourself at the annual State Fair of Texas in Dallas' historic Fair Park (bigtex.com; 214-565-9931).

State Fair Fried Foods
Dallas

The State Fair of Texas holds the title of the Fried Food Capital of Texas®—
and that's no idle boast. What began with Fletcher's Original State Fair
Corny Dogs back in 1942 (and, yep, you'll still find a long line for Fletcher's
Corny Dogs today) has now grown into a Texas-sized list of fried foods that
competitors attempt to top every year.

The entries get creative, tossing things into the boiling vat you'd never
dream could be deep fried. Winners in past years have grabbed the atten-
tion of judges with dishes that included:
  • Fried bubblegum
  • Fried Peaches and Cream
  • Fried Beer™
  • Fried Banana Split
  • Deep Fried Butter
  • Fried Coke
  • Fried PB, Jelly and Banana Sandwich
Hey, no one ever said it was the State Fair of Health Food…

Waterfall Billboard
Dallas

The 800-square-foot sign is equipped with a 35-foot-tall waterfall made out
of hay bales and plastic rocks. A pump circulates the water from a 10,000-
gallon tank. It overlooks the busy Stemmons Freeway. But some people think
it's the beach.

"The hardest part we have is keeping people off of it," said Arnold Velez
of Clear Channel Outdoor, the owner of the sign. "It's a landmark and people
say, 'Wouldn't it be cool if we went out there and went swimming in it?' I
can't imagine it. It's pretty grungy water." It's also one heck of a climb.

That doesn't stop them, though. "We've run people off who have been
sunbathing," Velez said. "People will just get on the rocks and act like they're
on a waterfall in Hawaii somewhere."

The waterfall dates back to 1962. PARIS PERMENTER AND JOHN BIGLEY

Sometimes during the weekend of the Texas-Oklahoma football game, the water gets a color job. If the OU fans get there first, it's dyed red; if the Texas fans beat them to it, the water turns up orange.

Old Rip
Eastland

Legend has it that during the 1897 dedication of the Eastland County Courthouse building in Eastland, Justice of the Peace Earnest Wood put a horned toad (nicknamed Old Rip) in a small hole chiseled in the cornerstone of the building. Then on February 28, 1928, when the courthouse was torn down to make room for another one, 3,000 people gathered on the courthouse square to see how Old Rip was doing.

Another Texas First

You've got to wonder if, in the beginning, teenagers hung out at Highland Park Village (hpvillage.com), commonly referred to as the first shopping center in the United States. When the center opened in 1931, was it an immediate magnet for teens, the way malls are today? Did they drive the security guards as nuts back then as they do today?

In 1931, architects Marion Fooshee and James Cheek began creating Highland Park Village in tony Highland Park, a small city surrounded by Dallas. It took more than twenty years to finish the shopping center, during which time construction was interrupted by the Great Depression and, later, World War II.

It would be several decades before the mall idea took off all over the United States. So, if it weren't for Highland Park Village, people all over the United States wouldn't be walking around mall parking lots right this minute, trying to find their cars.

After the horned toad was brought out of the hole, Judge Ed S. Pritchard held the toad upside down by his tail for all to see, "and his leg twitched and he came alive," said Bette Armstrong, known around town as the Toad Lady. After that, the horned toad became famous, toured the United States, and met President Calvin Coolidge in Washington. Old Rip died on January 19, 1929, of pneumonia.

This tale is big stuff in Texas, where the horned toad is the state reptile.

Armstrong takes this Old Rip business to heart. She used to wear a costume of Old Rip that she made herself in parades, and she has appeared at an Easter egg hunt in the suit with the Easter bunny. She also visited schools in her horned toad suit.

"I just like Old Rip," she explained.

As if that tale weren't strange enough, Old Rip was back in the headlines in 1973 when his body, then on display at the courthouse, was stolen. An anonymous letter was received that the story of Old Rip was a hoax. When there was no reaction, the kidnapper must have had a change of heart and left the little lizard on the county fairgrounds.

Old Rip is remembered all around the town of Eastland. BILLY HATHORN/CC-SA3.0

These days a deceased horned toad is back on display in a little plush-lined casket at the courthouse. So if his leg twitches again, we'll have a real news story.

The National Cowgirl Museum and Hall of Fame
Fort Worth

The first thing you notice when you walk into the National Cowgirl Museum and Hall of Fame (1720 Gendy St.; 817-336-4475) is the horse with a cowgirl hanging onto its neck coming out of the ceiling over by the gift shop.

That's a re-creation of Wild West show rider Mamie Hafley, who dove on her horse, Lurlene, from a fifty-foot platform into a ten-foot pool of water. She did this more than 640 times from 1908 to 1914, mostly during shows on the East Coast.

If either the cowgirl or her horse got hurt, it's not documented.

Giddyap! NATIONAL COWGIRL MUSEUM AND HALL OF FAME

Animal rights activists need not get fired up, either. Apparently the horse enjoyed the stunt more than the rider.

"The interesting story is Lurlene absolutely loved it and Mamie could not swim," said Susan Fine, the Cowgirl Museum and Hall of Fame's former marketing and development director. "So she would hang onto Lurlene's neck until they came back up."

The Hall of Fame, located in a $21 million building, has 220 honorees of various sorts, such as writer Willa Cather, horse opera queen Dale Evans, Lewis and Clark guide Sacagawea, country singer Patsy Cline, artist Georgia O'Keeffe, and former Supreme Court Justice Sandra Day O'Connor.

"She was a rancher and a trail blazer in her own right," Fine said of O'Connor. "She grew up on a ranch—the Lazy B. She drove cattle."

It's a fun museum because of all the interactive stuff. You can get your picture taken and have it made into a Western movie poster that you can pick up later in the gift shop. You can ride on a Plexiglas bronc on a spring and get a ten-second video made of you riding the thing, then download it from the museum's website (cowgirl.net).

You're a What?

If you attend Itasca High, you're a Wampus Cat. That's the school mascot. The cat part everybody can figure out. It's the wampus part that throws folks off.

According to school secretary Diane Barnes, a wampus cat is a fierce, supernatural Indian-legend critter that's half man, half cat.

"We've got like a fault line outside of town with little hills, and the kids say, 'You know, I saw a wampus cat out there,' but nobody knows what that means because nobody's caught one," she said. "There's really no such thing, but we won't tell anybody that."

So how did the school come up with this name? "There's two different stories," Barnes said. "They got the name back in the 1920s, and it was either a cheerleader that named it or a football player." One story has Itasca High football player Travis Burks crowing after a successful football game, "Boy, we played like wampus cats tonight." And the other story has cheerleader Donna Farrow picking the winning name in a contest to come up with a mascot for the school.

"Since both of those people are dead, it's kinda hard to prove it," said Barnes, herself a Wampus Cat since she graduated from Itasca High. "It's hard to explain, but it's a great nickname," Barnes said.

By the way, the name of the high school yearbook is *The Mowana*. Barnes admitted she had no idea what that means. "We don't have any usual names around here," she said. "Everything's got to be weird."

Check out the horse head over the Reel Cowgirls Theater upstairs, where you can see a retrospective about cowgirls in the movies. The horse interacts with the film; his head, eyes, and lips move as he talks. A note, though, that the museum will close its second floor exhibits starting February 2018 for a $5.5 million renovation, and will reopen in February 2019 with new galleries that expand upon the bond between women, horses, and the West through many Cowgirl Hall of Fame Honorees.

World's Largest Cedar Rocking Chair
Lipan

It was the world's largest rocking chair when it was listed in the *Guinness Book of World Records 2003*. Since then, a battle of the big chairs has produced at least four others challenging the claim, but the Star of Texas rocker still holds the record as the largest cedar rocking chair in the world. This colossal chair stands in front of Texas Hill Country Furniture and Mercantile (txhcountry.com; 254-646-3376) at 19280 S. Hwy 281, five miles south of I-20.

What began as a rustic home-furnishings store has morphed into an entire conglomerate of outbuildings including a smokehouse serving up tasty smoked meats (254-646-3844), a blacksmith shop offering sturdy hand-forged items, a custom leather shop, sawmill, old corncrib, and more. The mercantile store itself displays an amazing collection of fine furnishings, handmade crafts, and accent pieces.

Oh, yes . . . back to the rocking chair. Owner Larry Dennis said a shopper once showed him a photo of a large rocker. He immediately saw the attention-getting potential of it, so he decided to build one even bigger from the large cedar logs he used for his custom furniture. In five and a half days, his team created this behemoth, weighing 5,672 pounds and measuring 25 feet and 10 ½ inches tall and 12 feet and 7.37 inches wide.

How do I get up there? THE CAROUSELAMBRA KID/FLICKR.COM

Washing Machine Museum
Mineral Wells

Fred Wilson isn't cleaning up on his collection of old washing machines on display in his Washing Machine Museum at The Laumdronat, located at 700 W. Hubbard St. (940-328-1662). This is because he doesn't charge admission. Economists would probably go round and round with Wilson on this practice, but let's cut the puns and spin over to some actual information about the museum.

Wilson started his collection by buying an old wooden washing machine. "I had so much fun showing it to people, and one thing led to another," he said. Wilson has close to fifty old machines; the oldest dating back to about 1885. Wilson buys the machines in antiques malls and shops.

Trace the history of the washing machine at this unique museum.
MINERAL WELLS CHAMBER OF COMMERCE

"I treat myself to a new one every month or two," he said. "After spending so much money, you just keep spending it and quit worrying about it."

The collection includes various brands you've never heard of, such as Pohr, Minute Wash, and Easy Wash, and some brands you have heard of, including Black & Decker. I didn't know Black & Decker made a washing machine. "I didn't, either," Wilson said.

Some of Wilson's washing machines don't look like washing machines. One of them is a wooden barrel with a crank on the side. "I bought it down in Houston," he said. "I thought it was a butter churn. And another one I bought, I thought it was a pressure cooker."

Either way, Wilson's hobby is unique. "There's not many washing machine collectors," he said. "I've found one in West Virginia and Denver, I believe."

And, if all this inspires you to do a little laundry, you're in luck: The Laumdronat is a coin-operated laundromat or, as would be more commonly said here in Texas, a washateria.

Moo-La
Stephenville

This is dairy cattle country, so the people here milk it for all it's worth.

As you drive past the Erath County Courthouse, you'll see Moo-La, the fiberglass Holstein installed in 1972 to thank the area's dairy cows for all of

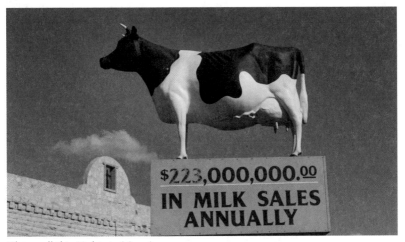

They call this Holstein Moo-La.

THE LYDA HILL TEXAS COLLECTION OF PHOTOGRAPHS IN CAROL M. HIGHSMITH'S AMERICA PROJECT, LIBRARY OF CONGRESS, PRINTS AND PHOTOGRAPHS DIVISION.

the mulah they have brought to the area—$223,000,000 IN MILK SALES ANNU-ALLY, says the sign on Moo-La. That's a lot of milk mustaches.

Below Moo-La, at ground level, there's a plaque honoring the Erath County 4-H dairy judging team, which in 1997 won the dairy-judging national championship at Madison, Wisconsin. This was the seventy-sixth annual contest, so when the team of Stephenville High School students became the first Texas team to win the national title, it was a major breakthrough. So major, in fact, that the plaque has a quote on it about overcoming adversity from the late Casey Stengel, the famous manager of the New York Yankees and a master of double-talk. THEY SAY YOU CAN'T DO IT, BUT REMEMBER, THAT DOESN'T ALWAYS WORK, reads the Stengel quote.

Dung Beetle Sculpture
Strawn

A dung beetle isn't the kind of insect you would think would make sellable art. After all, this is a bug that rolls up animal dung into a ball and lays its eggs in the ball so the larvae can feed on it. Neither is this the sort of thing you would expect to make a great high school mascot.

Still, Marc Rankin makes artwork dung beetles out of scrap metal that he finds in salvage yards—and a school has adopted one of them as its own.

"The junkyard is [Marc's] favorite place to hang," said his wife, Lisa, who doesn't know a lot about dung beetles. "Marc knows what there is to know about 'em," she said. "I just know they roll little turds up." Isn't that enough?

So far Marc has built about seven dung beetles. Each has two parts—the actual bug and the ball of poop that the bug rolls around. One of Marc's metal insects is the world's largest dung beetle, according to Lisa, at 6 feet tall and 4 ½ feet wide with a dung ball 48 inches in diameter. It was bought by a business in Granbury for $1,800.

Not all of the dung beetles are large. Lisa said a teacher in Houston called and ordered a small, desk-sized dung beetle so that the school principal's face could be placed on the dung ball. The teacher who ordered it even sent a photo of the principal for the artwork.

"Apparently, the principal has no kind of sense of humor," Lisa said.

So why make dung beetle sculptures? Marc said it's because they are Texana. "People in Texas are proud of Texas, and they really do like that kind of stuff," he said. But there's a more practical reason.

"Somebody asked for one," Lisa said. "That was how he started making 'em. Somebody asked if he could make a dung beetle, and he said, 'Yeah, I guess I can.'"

What's That You Say?

Sam Houston and Mirabeau B. Lamar, two of the four presidents of the Republic of Texas, hated each other's guts.

"Part of it was personal animosity," said Dick Rice, historical interpreter of the Sam Houston Museum in Huntsville. Part of it was diverging viewpoints on issues. "They had a completely different view on the Indians," Rice said. "Houston had supported the Cherokees north of Nacogdoches. And Lamar ran 'em out."

Suffice it to say that the two men did not get along. So at Lamar's inauguration as the president of the Republic of Texas in 1838, outgoing president Houston decided to gum up the show.

Houston showed up for the occasion dressed up in a silly outfit that was "elaborate" and "mostly green, with gold trim," Rice said. The outfit included a green cap, which the museum has on display. Houston then proceeded to give a speech that supposedly went on for three hours. The story has it that Houston was so long-winded that Lamar never got a chance to speak at his own inauguration.

Today Rankin's largest dung beetle sculpture—along with Rankin's sculpture of Killer, the world's largest armadillo—can be seen near Granbury at Fall Creek Farms (6921 Fall Creek Highway, Acton), a pick-your-own farm that opens several times a year to the public.

The Solitary Smokestack
Thurber

"What's that big, tall thing up ahead?"

Driving along I-20 about seventy miles west of Fort Worth, it's hard to miss the 128-foot brick smokestack towering above the rolling hills. Thurber was once a thriving town of 5,000 to 8,000 people, the largest city between Fort Worth and El Paso. But the smokestack is almost all that remains of this ghost town (population: 5).

The little town has a colorful history, told by eight Texas historical markers. Founded around 1888, it was a company town controlled by the Texas and Pacific Coal Company, later the Texas Pacific Oil Company. During boom times, Thurber mines produced 3,000 tons of coal a day! The coal deposits helped the railroads open the Southwest, and rich clay deposits made Thurber a huge producer of quality bricks that paved hundreds of miles of Texas streets and roads.

Thurber was also an interesting place because of its ethnic diversity. It was a true melting pot of coal miners and brick makers from around the world, speaking several languages. The majority were Italians, who were responsible for constructing the 650-seat opera house.

A progressive community, Thurber was the first totally electrified town in the United States. Every home had elec-

Thurber's smokestack is lonely but historic.
NICOLAS HENDERSON/FLICKR.COM

tricity and running water. The smokestack was part of the power plant built in 1895, cutting-edge technology for its time.

But when oil was discovered just down the road near Ranger and railroads switched from coal to oil . . . well, that was pretty much the end of Thurber. Today, the Smokestack Restaurant (smokestack.net; 254-672-5560), in one of the original brick buildings, is a popular place to stop between Fort Worth and Abilene.

Munster House
Waxahachie

Sandra McKee is such a huge fan of the 1960s TV horror send-up *The Munsters* that she decided to build a new house that looked just like the one on the show. Now she's living in the 5,825-square-foot mansion with her husband, Charles.

McKee came up with the design for the interior of the house by rewatching episodes of the show. "It's amazing how much you have to research when you're doing a project like this," she said.

Oh, it's not an exact replica. The kitchen looks pretty normal. "I couldn't do one like theirs 'cause they had cabinets falling down, and I didn't want cabinets falling down 'cause I'd have to live here," McKee said.

The suit of armor at the top of the stairs rotates like the one on the TV show, and the creepy stairs leading up to it rise eerily with the help of pneumatic equipment.

The dungeon was a challenge. "We don't have a basement, since this is the 100-year floodplain," McKee said. "So we had to get a storm shelter and sink it so we could have a dungeon. 'Course, we did get in it a few weeks ago when we had tornado warnings around here."

McKee is a Munsters nut. She watches the reruns twice a day on TV—at 8:30 in the morning and at 10:30 at night. "There's some shows I love more than others," she said. "And even if I can't watch it, I love to have it on and hear it. I dunno. It's relaxing to me." She owns all seventy episodes of the series, whose main characters—the Munster family—were a collection of horror-movie rejects.

"They're just an average American family," she said. "Herman went to work. Lily was the housewife. Eddie went to school. Marilyn went to college. They were a very honest, clean family. They never hurt people. They just ate different things." Like what? "They had, like, centipede salad and yak," she answered.

She and Charles started building the place in 2001, and they moved into the house in 2002. On Halloween 2002 they had a big Munsters party. Al Lewis, who played Grandpa Munster, and Butch Patrick, who played Eddie Munster, were invited and showed up, along with 500 to 600 other folks in costume.

"[Lewis] actually had tears in his eyes when he came inside," McKee said. "He said it brought back a lot of memories." Oh, that downstairs closet

Sandra McKee built her new house to look just like the one on the 1960s TV horror send-up. PARIS PERMENTER AND JOHN BIGLEY

door that appears to be made out of a coffin isn't really made out of a coffin. "A funeral home wanted to donate a coffin, but I said nah," Sandra said. "They said, 'You'd get used to it,' but I said, 'I don't want to get used to it.' I don't want to come downstairs and see a coffin sitting there."

The one and only time folks can see inside the mansion is during the annual Halloween bash, a charity fund-raiser. The public can take pictures from the themed gate by driving past 1313 Mockingbird Lane. See the house at munstermansion.com.

Peter Pan Statue
Weatherford

According to *Peter Pan*, "Dreams do come true, if only we wish hard enough. You can have anything in life if you will sacrifice everything else for it."

Well, if you're wishing you could meet Peter Pan, the next best thing just might be a stop at the Peter Pan statue in Weatherford. Located in front of

Neiman Marcus Cookie Yarn

Legend has it that a woman liked the chocolate chip cookies at the tony Dallas department store's restaurant so much that she asked for the recipe. The waitress gave it to her. The story goes that the woman later got a charge for $250 on her credit card. In some versions of the story, it's a Visa credit card.

Neiman Marcus points out that when the story first made the rounds, the company only took its own card and American Express.

In fact, Neiman Marcus didn't even serve cookies in its restaurants until after this urban legend began circulating years ago.

Anyway, here's the recipe, straight from the store:

Makes 12-15 large cookies

Ingredients:

½ cup unsalted butter, softened

1 cup brown sugar

3 tablespoons granulated sugar

1 egg

2 teaspoons vanilla extract

½ teaspoon baking soda

½ teaspoon baking powder

½ teaspoon salt

1¾ cups of flour

1½ teaspoons instant espresso powder, slightly crushed

8 ounces semisweet chocolate chips

Cream the butter with the sugars until fluffy. Beat in the egg and the vanilla extract. Combine the dry ingredients and beat into the butter mixture. Stir in the chocolate chips. Drop large spoonfuls onto a greased cookie sheet. Bake at 375°F for 8-10 minutes, or 10-12 minutes for a crisper cookie.

If you use this recipe, you will be billed by the authors of this book at the rate of $250 per cookie.

Just kidding.

You can fly! PARIS PERMENTER AND JOHN BIGLEY

the Weatherford Public Library (1014 Charles St.), the life-sized bronze statue by Ronald Thomason depicts Weatherford native Mary Martin (mother of actor Larry Hagman) during her days as Broadway's rendition of Peter Pan, the mischievous boy who never grows up.

Wichita Falls Waterfall
Wichita Falls

You're next to US 287 with traffic whizzing by. You have just walked down a wooded trail decorated with a sign that warns you it's against the law to leave dog poop behind. Above you, although you can't see it from your vantage point, is a cemetery.

Where are you?

The best waterfall money can buy WICHITA FALLS CONVENTION AND VISITORS BUREAU

You are standing at the base of the Wichita Falls Waterfall, a man-made waterfall that was turned on June 5, 1987, by Michael O'Laughlin who at the time was Mayor of Niagara Falls (wichitafallstx.gov/75/The-Falls).

If O'Laughlin had gone over these falls in a barrel, he probably would have survived. The four-tiered waterfall, constructed of rocks, is fifty-four feet high. A seventy-five-horsepower pump circulates water out of the muddy, red Wichita River for the falls.

The falls cost $418,817 to put in, $230,000 of which was donated by folks and businesses.

Why such a crying need for a falls? See, the real waterfall for which the town was named was washed away by a flood in 1886. So the town needed another falls. Otherwise, the name of the place might have to be changed to Wichita Flats. Visit wichitafalls.org for more Wichita Falls travel info.

The "world's littlest skyscraper". WICHITA FALLS CONVENTION AND VISITORS BUREAU

World's Littlest Skyscraper
Wichita Falls

I couldn't find anyone to verify the legend behind this tiny building at 7th and LaSalle Streets in the city's historic district.

The story goes that the "skyscraper" was the result of an oil boom scam in the early part of the twentieth century, according to Carole Woessner of the Wichita County Heritage Society.

Oil had been struck in nearby Burkburnett, prompting people to flood the area to seek their fortunes. Meanwhile, back in New York, the newspapers were reporting a shortage of office space in Wichita Falls, and a prospectus began circulating that offered stock in a skyscraper to be built in Wichita Falls.

A drawing of the would-be building showed it reaching into the sky, dwarfing other buildings. Supposedly, $200,000 in stock was sold to build it. The story goes on to say that in 1919 the little building was built by J. D. McMahon, a construction engineer from Philadelphia. McMahon avoided legal problems by building the building to scale—in inches instead of feet. McMahon then quickly left Wichita Falls.

Regardless of how it got here, the brick, tower-shaped building is nearly 17 feet deep by 10 feet wide by 40 feet high—and too small for an office. Woessner said it doesn't even have a stairwell.

East Texas

For those of you who grew up watching old Wild West movies, we hate to disillusion you, but not all of Texas is covered in cacti and tumbleweeds. East Texas contains lush forests, fertile soil, and rolling hills. Northeastern Texas is a showplace of flowering dogwoods and azaleas in spring, Tyler roses in summer, and glorious color in autumn.

Also called Deep East Texas or the Piney Woods, this area of tall pine forests is dotted with dozens of lakes noted for superb fishing. The historic and mysterious Caddo Lake is the only natural lake in Texas. Encompassing about 26,800 acres, it straddles the border with Louisiana and is lined with magnificent old cypress trees draped in Spanish moss. Farther south, the area known as the Big Thicket is dominated by wetlands and swamps, ecologically different from the rest of the region.

Stretching from the northeast corner and running parallel to its borders with Oklahoma, Arkansas, and Louisiana nearly to the Gulf of Mexico, this area includes College Station, home of Texas A&M University and the George Bush Presidential Library. Washington County is the "birthplace of Texas history."

This book includes Texas's largest city, Houston, in this region. With a metropolitan-area population of nearly 6 million, many of them young people and folks from other places, Houston is a hodgepodge of cultures and ethnic groups, magnificent museums and attractions, incredible restaurants, and NASA's Lyndon B. Johnson Space Center.

Yes, East Texas has its share of curiosities, too.

Mount Aggie
College Station

Leave it to the Aggies to be at the leading edge of the unusual. Is this the only ski slope in Texas?

"I can't really answer that; it's the only one I know of," said Frank Thomas, chairman of Texas A&M University's physical education activity program.

It's the only one I've ever heard of. Mount Aggie—actually, Mount Aggie IV—is an artificial ski slope for beginning and intermediate snow skiing, two of the most popular physical education courses at Texas A&M.

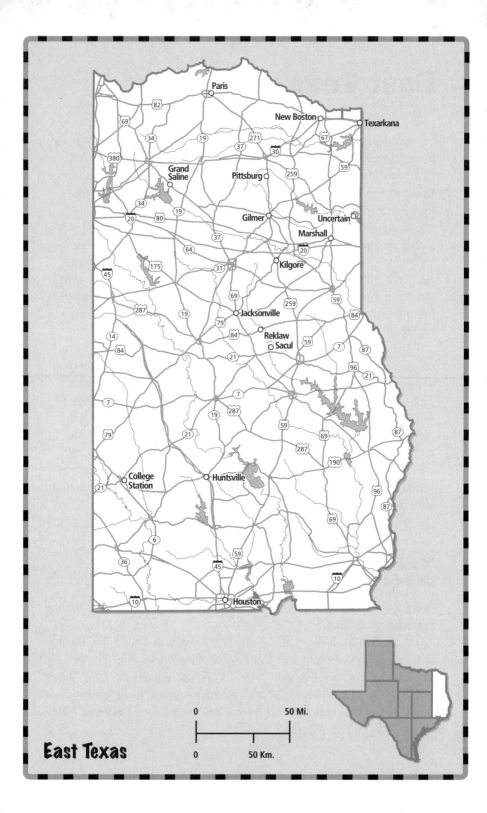

East Texas

What's in a Name?

Surprisingly, Texas didn't get its name because it fits well on a bumper sticker. It just worked out that way.

This Texas business started when early Spanish settlers met the Hasinai Caddo Indians of East Texas. The Hasinais used the word *tayshas*, meaning "friends" or "allies," as a greeting. In Spanish the word came out *tejas*, which eventually became Texas. How "howdy" came along is another matter, however. And why Texans call oil "all" is yet another.

That *Texas* means "friends," though, is fitting, because this is a friendly state. In West Texas it's customary for people to wave at each other from their trucks, even if they don't know each other. This is often done with the one-hand wave—a wave accomplished by lifting the fingers of the hand without letting go of the steering wheel.

In Austin, drivers are more likely to give a different kind of one-finger salute, but it's a big state, and it has its cultural differences.

Located on West Campus next to Swine Center, Mount Aggie IV is not the kind of slope to set you to yodeling. But it is 73 feet high, 150 feet wide and 520 feet long. The slope, a pile of dirt with a concrete base, is lined on top with an Astroturf-type surface and lubricated for downhill runs by a sprinkler system. Sadly, it does not come with a Saint Bernard carrying a tiny keg under its neck.

Mount Aggie IV is a far cry from the original Mount Aggie that was 21 feet high and had two 90-foot runs. Thomas said that before it was torn down, the original Mount Aggie was a popular spot for Aggies to bring visitors from out of town to show them that you can ski in College Station. Along with its use by students, Mount Aggie is also available for private rentals for sledding parties.

The Deceased Mascot Flap

The Texas A&M Aggies are as serious as a case of the hives about their traditions, and they have more of them than a used car lot has salesmen in cheap suits.

It's a tradition for the Aggies to stand up during football games. It's a tradition for the guys to kiss the gals in the stands after A&M touchdowns. It's a tradition for the Corps of Cadets to wear burr haircuts. Traditionally, the male cheerleaders are called "yell leaders."

So it should have been no big surprise in the summer of 1997 that some Aggies were outraged when the graves of four of their deceased canine mascots were moved across the street from Kyle Field, the football stadium, and reburied next to the statue of the Twelfth Man (another A&M tradition that says the fans in the stands at football games are the "twelfth man" on the field for A&M). The four Reveilles—three Collies and a mixed breed former stray—were relocated for the $30 million expansion of Kyle Field.

The reason some were miffed when the dogs were moved from a place near the stadium to a spot across the street? Tradition at A&M says the dogs are to be buried paws and faces pointing toward the stadium's north tunnel so they can see the scoreboard inside the stadium. And in their new location, the dogs' line of sight to the scoreboard was blocked, so they could no longer see the score.

To fix this, a small scoreboard that the dogs can see from their graves has been erected on the side of the stadium.

The East Texas Yamboree
Gilmer

Held the third Wednesday through Saturday in October, this four-day festival is for folks who have a hankering to decorate a yam.

The yam-decorating contest is for children, but "I guess adults could join it; I don't know," said Charlotte Denson, former secretary of the Gilmer Area Chamber of Commerce.

I yam what I yam. PARIS PERMENTER AND JOHN BIGLEY

What do the children decorate their yams to look like? "There's always a Dolly Parton, and there's always some whales, porpoises, penguins, [and] airplanes," Denson said. "Their imaginations run wild."

The festival, which Denson said attracts about 100,000 people each year, used to have a bicycle race called, you got it, the "Tour de Yam."

All right, I'll quit yammerin' on. Call the Gilmer Chamber at (903) 843-2413 for more information, or visit yamboree.com.

Don't Lick the Building
Grand Saline

The only building in North America made of pure rock salt sits in the middle of Grand Saline, home of one of the largest, purest salt domes in the country. Built in 1936 as part of the Texas Centennial Celebration, the original Salt Palace melted away and was eventually torn down. The community rebuilt a palace of local salt blocks (with a bit of mortar and other protective elements), in 1975 and again in 1993, and instituted the annual Grand Saline Salt Festival, held each June.

If you do lick the building you won't be the first!

Although visitors cannot tour the Morton Salt Company's mine itself, they can get a good feel for the mining operations in a video filmed in the 750-foot-deep underground mine and shown in the Grand Saline Salt Palace Museum and Visitors Center (100 W. Garland St.; grandsalinesaltpalace.com, 903-962-5631). The museum features historical photos and memorabilia of the salt industry along this part of historic US 80 dating from 1845. Each visitor receives a complimentary salt crystal, so you really don't need to lick the walls.

The Beer Can House
Houston

From 1968 to 1988, the late John Milkovisch covered his entire house at 222 Malone St. with flattened beer cans, said his son Ronald.

Dad, an upholsterer for the Southern Pacific Railroad, was a big beer drinker who generally kept eight cases of beer in the garage, Ronald recalled. "He even had a Shiner distributor stop by once and ask if he wanted beer delivered."

The house is covered with flattened beer cans, except for some spaces up under the eaves. John Milkovisch developed a method that involved making panels of fifteen beer cans each. Then the panels were tacked to the house, label side out, so you could tell what he'd been drinking.

Many of the labels you'll see on the house are discount brands, some of which don't exist anymore: Texas Pride, Pabst Blue Ribbon, Jax, Falstaff, Buckhorn, and Southern Select. "He used any beer that was on special, just to try to save a dime, 'cause he bought a lot of beer," Ronald said.

The project began when John Milkovisch made strings of beer can tops to dangle in front of the west and south sides of his house to keep the

This is one of Houston's folk art masterpieces—a home covered in 50,000 beer cans and tabs. VISITHOUSTON

steamy Houston sun off it. "There was an ulterior motive, other than being eccentric and a little bit crazy," Ronald said.

The strings of can tops used to tinkle merrily in the breeze, but the pop top strings have been removed because of hurricanes. Wouldn't want to lose those in a high wind. "But it's cool because you get to see what's underneath those things, and that's aluminum siding twelve ounces at a time," said Allen Hill, previously media and marketing coordinator for the Orange Show Center for Visionary Art.

The art foundation purchased the Beer Can House and restored it. The last person to live in the house was the late Mary Milkovisch, John Milkovisch's widow. Even the mailbox is covered with beer cans—in this case, Bud Light. So you could say that no surface has been left uncanned (beercanhouse.org). Now a permanent part of the Orange Show, it's open to visitors. See it at orangeshow.org.

The Orange Show
Houston

Starting in the mid-1950s, the late Jeff McKissack, a Houston mailman, collected wagon wheels, tile, rocks, hunks of metal, and other junk found on his downtown delivery route. Then he built a monument out of it, which he called the Orange Show.

McKissack thought the orange was the perfect food. Hence, the name. The junk, however, has made the magical leap to art. Today the Orange Show Center for the Visionary Arts (orangeshow.org; 2402 Munger St., 713-926-6368), a nonprofit arts organization with a $1 million annual budget, looks after it, teaches art classes in it, and conducts tours of it.

You could say the Orange Show has moved from the dump to docents.

At one time McKissack considered building a plant nursery, a worm farm, or a beauty salon on the site. These days, the place has a lot of whirligigs that make noise, and you can sit in tractor seats McKissack found to watch a working steam engine.

The Orange Show Center for the Visionary Arts puts on the world's oldest and longest art-car parade on the second weekend of May, featuring decorated cars, such as Richard Carter's spectacular Sashimi Tabernacle Choir, a mid-1980s model Volvo covered with roughly 250 singing fish and lobsters. "You remember those annoying singing fish that were popular at Christmas?" Carter asked. "That's pretty much the foundation."

Carter, who works for an engineering company, settled on the singing fish car idea because "it was too good to pass up," he said. "I knew I

More than 250,000 spectators line downtown's streets to view this parade, which showcases Houston's most outlandish folk art creations on wheels.
VISITHOUSTON

somehow had to make it happen." So, he bought a bunch of singing fish and lobsters at a Walgreens drugstore. "The clerks really loved me there," he recalled. "They wanted me to buy more so they wouldn't have to listen to the damn things." He said his fish and lobsters sing everything from the theme song for the TV show *Rawhide* to a couple of operatic numbers.

The National Museum of Funeral History
Houston

If things are a little dead, why not stop in at the National Museum of Funeral History?

Opened in 1992, the museum (nmfh.org; 415 Barren Springs Dr., 281-876-3063) shares the building with a school for morticians and boasts "fantasy coffins" from Ghana in the shapes of a Mercedes, a chicken, a bull, a fish, an outboard motor, a lobster, a KLM jet, and a shallot, to name a few.

The sign said the airplane would be a casket "for someone who had never flown." You'd think it would be the other way around.

Are we having fun yet? VISITHOUSTON

"That shallot would be for a family that raised onions and sold them in an open-air market," explained Gary L. Sanders, a mortician by trade and the museum's former director.

The museum's motto? "Any Day Above Ground Is a Good One." Visitors to the museum—about 6,000 people a year visit the place—can buy baseball caps and coffee cups decorated with that chirpy reminder.

Any interactive exhibits? Nope. "We try to keep it in good taste; that's our deal," Sanders said.

Among the more interesting exhibits? Check out the Packard Funeral Bus, one of many funeral vehicles on display. Built circa 1916, the bus was used just once—in a funeral in San Francisco. It was hauling the casket, the pallbearers, and twenty mourners. When it tipped back from the weight, the pallbearers fell over the mourners, and the casket overturned.

Holy Smoke
Huntsville

The official name of the church at 2601 Montgomery Road (936-295-2349) is the New Zion Missionary Baptist Church. But it's better known as the Church of the Holy Smoke.

This is because of the barbecue business right next door to the church with the barrel-shaped cooker out front. Sometimes there is so much oak wood smoke pouring out of the cooker that it looks like somebody ought to call the fire department.

This all started back in the mid-1970s when some of the deacons were painting the church. "The ladies went out to fix dinner, and they had this old pit they started a fire on," said the Rev. Clint Edison, the church pastor. "And they was just making a day out of cleaning the church."

The aroma from the fire and the meat cooking began attracting passersby. "And people began to stop and ask was they selling barbecue," Rev. Edison said. "They said they couldn't even fix their husbands dinner for people asking if they were selling barbecue."

The next week, Rev. Edison said some of the church members borrowed $50 from the church to buy meat, then started up a barbecue business. "And it's been going ever since," he said.

At first the barbecue business didn't even have a building. "They just had a pit outside," said Horace Archie, who helps run both the church's Sunday school and the barbecue operation.

Barbecue is sold Thursday through Saturday. The barbecue isn't going on Sunday because it could be a distraction to the flock next door at the church. "When you're smelling food, your mind drifts," Horace explained.

You can order pork ribs, chicken, beef brisket, and sausage. Order by the pound, by the plate, or go Texas-sized with an all-you-can-eat platter for $20 (936-294-0884).

The little barbecue building isn't much to look at. A small, handmade poster out front tells the hours of operation and says MAY GOD BLESS YOU. A bench near the cooker consists of a warped piece of plywood set on top of a couple of stumps. Inside, you'll sit at long picnic tables that have advertisements for local businesses laminated on top: Oliphant's Furniture, CP Electronics, the Mattress Factory. Each place setting comes with two pieces of white bread wrapped in cellophane. The barbecue is heavy with sauce, which explains why you'll find rolls of paper towels on every table.

When Sam Houston State is playing a home football game, sometimes the visiting team will show up to eat. One time it was about thirty-five guys

There's no barbecue on Sunday; don't want to distract anyone.
JASON P./FLICKR.COM

from the McNeese State squad, Horace recalled. Did they eat him out of business? "They didn't clean us out, but they got close," he said.

On some Sunday mornings the barbecue place puts on a Bible quiz for a prize. This consists of Horace or another church member asking a Bible question on one of the local radio stations. "Whoever answers the question gets a meat plate," Horace said. A picture of some of the contest winners decorates one of the restaurant walls.

But you don't have to be of a religious bent to eat in here. "There's some regular Hell's Angels that come by in the summer," Horace said. "They didn't do no cuttin' up."

Texas Prison Museum
Huntsville

The Texas Prison Museum (txprisonmuseum.org; 491 Hwy. 75 N., 936-295-2155) is an unusual museum, to say the least. The centerpiece is Old Sparky, the oak electric chair that went out of business in 1964 after zapping 361 death-row dwellers over the course of forty years.

Old Sparky isn't plugged in, by the way. This is not an interactive exhibit. Children are discouraged from climbing on Old Sparky, even though that photo would make a great Christmas card, huh? On the other hand, you can put on a black-and-white–striped jacket available at the museum and get your picture snapped behind bars in the 6-by-9-foot cell, just like the one Texas prison inmates live in.

Senior citizens who stop in to visit just love doing that, according to Janice Willett, previously the museum's treasurer. "They wear these shirts, and they just think it's hilarious," she said.

Just like in real prison, a toilet sits right out in the open inside the cell, providing absolutely no privacy but a great opportunity for an unusual Christmas card photo. "We get these high school kids in here all the time, and they want to get [pictures of] their friends sitting on the toilet," said Jim Willett, the museum director and a former warden of the state prison system's Walls Unit.

Old Sparky is the museum's top exhibit. TEXAS PRISON MUSEUM

The museum moved into an 8,000-square-foot building in 2002 after being in a much smaller space on the Walker County Courthouse Square. Moving the museum cost about $l million, and you can't miss the location. It's the place with the guard tower out front, near I-45 (exit 118).

This museum ironically has been visited over the years by some former prison inmates who have dropped in to take a look. You mean these guys really come in on purpose? "Oh, absolutely," Janice Willett said. "When we were downtown, we were one block from the bus station. So when the parolees got out, they would come to the museum. That was a daily occurrence."

The place even has a souvenir shop. I was particularly fond of the striped T-shirt you can purchase that says, I DID TIME IN HUNTSVILLE. They also sell a shirt that says "PEN STATE."

Sam Houston Statue
Huntsville

The president of the Republic of Texas (1836–38 and 1841–44) is big in Huntsville, literally and figuratively.

The 60-foot, 30-ton statue of Sam Houston next to I-45 about two miles south of town is the world's largest free-standing figure of an American hero (huntsvilletexas .com/148/Statue-Visitor-Center). The white sculpture, done by Huntsville native David Adickes, is so big that you can see it from six and a half miles away from the south. Actually, it kind of makes Sam Houston look like Colonel Sanders.

This town is ate up with Sam Houston, who retired here after serving as Texas governor. The gift shop at the visitor center near the statue was selling Sam Houston throw rugs, miniatures of the Sam Houston statue, Sam Houston statue shot glasses, Sam Houston statue T-shirts, "I Saw Big Sam in Huntsville, Texas"

That's one tall Texan! THE LYDA HILL TEXAS COLLECTION OF PHOTOGRAPHS IN CAROL M. HIGHSMITH'S AMERICA PROJECT, LIBRARY OF CONGRESS, PRINTS AND PHOTOGRAPHS DIVISION.

bumper stickers, and a T-shirt that explains it all with this message on the front: It's a Texan thing. Y'all wouldn't understand.

If you look in the Huntsville phone book, you'll find listings for the Sam Houston Group, and the Sam Houston Antique Mall. Huntsville is also the home of Sam Houston State University, Sam Houston's gravesite, the Sam Houston home, and the Sam Houston Memorial Museum.

And They Call It the Rodeo

"The inmates really did like the thing," said former Texas prison system spokesman Larry Fitzgerald, speaking of the now-defunct Texas Prison Rodeo, a piece of Texas history that started up during the Depression and was canceled in 1987.

No wonder the inmates liked performing in their own rodeo. Not only did the cash prizes for bull riding, bareback bronc riding, and steer wrestling give the winners some spending money, but it also gave them something to do and provided them with a chance to escape. Around 1940, two inmates escaped from the prison thanks to the rodeo. The two stole some civilian clothes out of the prison laundry, mingled with the rodeo crowd, and eventually dropped down into the stands and fled.

"A guard who was standing around thought they were two civilians who were trying to sneak in," Fitzgerald said. The guard admonished the two men for not paying their way into the arena and shooed them off.

The rodeo, held in the 26,000-seat arena next to the Walls Unit in Huntsville, was billed as "The World's Wildest Show Behind Bars," Fitzgerald said. "Most of the guys came into it with nothing to lose. So they went all out."

One event featured a Bull Durham sack full of money tied to a bull's horns. "Whoever took the Bull Durham sack off the horns got to keep the money," Fitzgerald said.

During the rodeo's history, at least two inmate cowboys were killed in bucking bronco accidents. And during the 1956 rodeo, veteran inmate rodeo clown Snuffy Garrett was pitched about twenty feet over a fence by a bull, breaking three of Snuffy's ribs. Apparently, the bull didn't think he was funny.

The Tomato Bowl
Jacksonville

"The story is it was built as a WPA [Works Progress Administration] project in 1934," said Matt Montgomery, who does the radio color commentary from the sidelines on Friday nights at this stadium. "It still has the original stone walls around it. It's basically an old downtown stadium. There's horrible parking. But it's real tight, real cozy."

Named in a newspaper article as one of the top ten places in Texas to watch a high school football game, the Tomato Bowl (202 Austin St.), not just the only stadium in America named for a BLT ingredient, also comes with a lot of traditions. The railroad track runs behind the north end of the stadium, providing a perch for some of the locals to sit on so they can watch the game without paying to get in.

"But trains come by all the time, so they have to get up and move," said Deena Brand, Jacksonville High's secretary of athletics.

Three or four trains come by each game, Montgomery added.

The Tomato Bowl is rich in tradition (but not nutrition!). LARRY D. MOORE/FLICKR.COM

"The trains always honk and make a ruckus," he said. Whenever that happens, John "Skipper" Reese, a local character and a Tomato Bowl fixture, gets out there near the tracks and waves the train through by whipping his arm around like he's directing traffic.

"I always mention on the radio that tonight's train is directed by John Reese," said Montgomery, an investments advisor who played quarterback in the Tomato Bowl for the Jacksonville High Fightin' Indians.

Check out the totem pole with the ten lightbulbs out front of the stadium. "When we win, the whole team and the whole crowd go up after the ballgame and they put a blue light signaling a win on the totem pole," Montgomery said. "If we don't win, we obviously don't go out." After a loss, white lightbulbs go up—eventually. But not right after the game.

The name of the stadium comes from the 1930s and 1940s when Jacksonville was the self-proclaimed Tomato Capital of the World.

Hey, it beats the Zucchini Bowl, right?

If you can't get enough of tomatoes, plan a trip back to Jacksonville for TomatoFest (jacksonvilletexas.com/tomato-fest), an annual festival held the second Saturday in June. While there's no longer a Battle of San Tomato, you'll have the chance to watch a tomato-eating contest—not to mention tomato basketball and tomato golf.

Rangerette Showcase Museum
Kilgore

So what does it take to become a member of the Kilgore Rangerettes, America's first football halftime-show precision-drill team?

"You know what the common thread is?" asked Lynne Oberthier, the nice lady who was on duty in the museum on the Kilgore College campus. "They know how to smile and project to the public. But they do have to be able to get their foot up over their head."

She's talking about the famous kick-line routine the Kilgore Rangerettes have performed for over a half century at the Cotton Bowl in Dallas. To make it onto the team of seventy-two young women, you have to be able to lift your white boot above your hairdo.

The Rangerettes all have one other trait in common: As you will see from the photos that line the walls of the museum, most of them are pretty darned cute.

The museum centerpiece is a sixty-seat, seven-row theater where you can watch a movie about the history of the Rangerettes, who were formed in 1940. In the movie you see the Rangerettes dancing to the song "Can You Feel a Brand New Day." This movie has more syrup than the Aunt Jemima factory.

Perhaps the most famous Rangerette of them all? Alice Lon, Lawrence Welk's first Champagne Lady, was a Kilgore Rangerette.

The Rangerettes are permanently on center stage at the Rangerette Showcase in the Physical Education Complex of Kilgore College (rangerette .com; 1100 Broadway, 903-983-8273).

The Rangerettes formed the first football halftime-show precision-drill team.

THE LYDA HILL TEXAS COLLECTION OF PHOTOGRAPHS IN CAROL M. HIGHSMITH'S AMERICA PROJECT,
LIBRARY OF CONGRESS, PRINTS AND PHOTOGRAPHS DIVISION.

Marvin Zindler

On Friday night during his restaurant health report, the late Marvin Zindler was known to holler dramatically, "Sliiiiiiimmmme in the iccccccce machine."

The KTRK-TV consumer reporter bought about twelve huge, white pompadour hairpieces a year and wasn't shy about mentioning it. His TV delivery on the evening news was that of a preacher working a tent revival. He wore sapphire blue–tinted sunglasses and plantation-owner white suits. He ended each of his reports at 6:00 and 10:00 p.m. with the signature sign-off, "MARRRRRRR-VIN Zindler, EEEEEYE-Witness NEWSSSSS!"

Marvin was with the Houston station since 1973 and was not the guy you wanted in your face with a TV camera if you were a business owner who had jacked around a customer. He loved charging into an office with a camera, feigning righteous indignation, and getting people's money back. He was kinda like Mike Wallace with a rug.

But the flamboyant Zindler went down in Texas history as the man who closed the Chicken Ranch, the famous brothel in the small Fayette County town of La Grange. In 1973, when Zindler reported on his show what everybody in the state legislature already knew—that there was a whorehouse sixty-five miles east of the Capitol—it forced then-Governor Dolph Briscoe to shut down the place.

The Chicken Ranch became even more famous after it went out of business. The brothel was glorified in *The Best Little Whorehouse in Texas*, both a musical and a movie starring Dolly Parton and Burt Reynolds.

Comedian Dom DeLuise played Zindler in the movie. Zindler, not a bashful fellow, said he could have done a better job himself. "He was silly, all right," Zindler said. "But if I'd played me straight, that was even funnier than trying to be funny."

He had an unprecedented lifetime contract that he honored. Zindler died in 2007, continuing to work even in his last days from his hospital bed. The flamboyant TV personality is now a legend in Houston.

Fire Ant Festival
Marshall

Like any town in Texas, Marshall has a fire ant problem. But its festival to the biting bugs gives the town a leg up on a sequel.

"If we ever do get rid of 'em, we will do a memorial festival to them," said Pam Whisenant, former tourism director for the town of 25,000 people.

Held the second weekend in October, the Fire Ant Festival has a fire ant calling contest. "No one knows what a fire ant sound is or if they make a sound," Whisenant admitted. "But we decided people should make three different calls: one for food, one that's an alarm call, and one that's for mating. And it's pretty fun what they come up with."

Then, for the daring, there's the fire ant roundup. Contestants are provided with plastic milk jugs to put the fire ants in. The person who collects the most fire ants in two hours wins $150. "Which probably will cover some of their medical expenses," Whisenant commented.

Who counts the fire ants to see who wins? "We don't actually count them; we end up weighing them," Whisenant said. "I think the most we've gotten is ten ounces. You know the size of ants. That's a lot of fire ants."

Fire ant boogie! JACK CANSON FOR MARSHALL CHAMBER OF COMMERCE

Jim Bowie Statue
New Boston

No, the 8-foot-tall bronze of the Alamo hero in front of the Bowie County Courthouse (710 James Bowie Dr.) doesn't have a little pinch between its cheek and gum, like Walt Garrison suggested in the old TV ad for Skoal chewing tobacco. But the knife-toting statue of Bowie, who died defending the Alamo, is done in the likeness of the long-since retired Dallas Cowboys running back.

"Walt Garrison did pose for it," said former Bowie County Judge Ed Miller. So the statue is wearing Jim Bowie clothes but has Walt Garrison's chiseled visage.

Miller said the statue caused him some amusing embarrassment. When a reporter for the *Texarkana Gazette* was interviewing him about the upcoming unveiling, Miller said he used the term "the erection of the James Bowie statue." Miller said it showed up that way in the newspaper "in heavy print."

Miller said his choice of words led to a call from a friend of his who was a member of the Daughters of the American Revolution. "She said they were going to have pilgrimages to the statue," Miller said.

Former Dallas Cowboy Walt Garrison modeled for this statue of Texas hero Jim Bowie. QUESTER MARK/FLICKR CC-BY-SA 2.0

Eiffel Tower Replica
Paris

Unlike the 984-foot-tall original in France, the 65-foot-tall Eiffel Tower (2025 S. Collegiate Dr.) in this Texas town doesn't have an elevator you can ride up to the top.

In fact, you are not even allowed to get on this Eiffel Tower. DO NOT CLIMB ON EIFFEL TOWER. IT IS AN UNSAFE ACTIVITY, the sign says. On the other hand, the original in France doesn't have a huge red cowboy hat on top, either.

The idea to build an Eiffel Tower cropped up in the mid-1990s, when Gary Vest became director of the Lamar County Chamber of Commerce. "Kind of facetiously, I started asking everybody, 'Well, where's our Eiffel Tower?'" he recalled.

Vest began talking about an Eiffel Tower with Rick Thomas, then plant manager at the Babcock & Wilcox boiler plant. Members of Boilermakers Local No. 902 built the tower for nothing out of scrap materials at the plant. Later, Daon Wall, who used to have a company called Wall Concrete Pipe, told Vest, "I'm gonna build that hat for you."

The 1,300-pound steel tower went up in 1996, and the hat was added in 1998.

Other than the Eiffel Tower and Culbertson Fountain downtown, there isn't much French in this town about ten miles south of the Oklahoma line. I looked around for a French restaurant, and all I could find was Le Colonel Sanders, Le Waga Bag, and Le Long John Silver's. So I ended up dining at a barbecue place that has—yes, french fries.

Ezekiel Airship
Pittsburg

In 1902, a year before the Wright Brothers got off the ground, a bizarre aircraft designed by Baptist preacher Burrell Cannon flew here—but not very well.

"According to the witnesses who saw it, it went up about ten feet and drifted about one hundred feet, and it was vibrating pretty bad, so they brought it down," said D. H. Abernathy, the mayor of Pittsburg for fifty-two years, from 1954 to 2006.

The Ezekiel Airship is so called because Reverend Cannon got the idea to build it from passages in the Old Testament book of Ezekiel that mention flight: "And when the living creatures went, the wheels went by them; and when the living creatures were lifted up from the earth, the wheels were lifted up."

Paris, Texas, may not have any French restaurants, but it does have this sixty-five-foot Eiffel Tower—topped with a Texas-size cowboy hat.

THE LYDA HILL TEXAS COLLECTION OF PHOTOGRAPHS IN CAROL M. HIGHSMITH'S AMERICA PROJECT,

LIBRARY OF CONGRESS, PRINTS AND PHOTOGRAPHS DIVISION.

This prompted Reverend Cannon to raise money to build an airship. In 1900, a group gathered in the local opera house to create the Ezekiel Airship Company. Stock was sold for $25 a share, and $20,000 was raised to build the ship.

The work was done on the second floor of the Pittsburg Foundry and Machine Shop. Mayor Abernathy said the ship was so big that they had to tear out part of the south wall to get it out of the building.

Perhaps the airship's longest flight occurred in 1903, when a tornado blew it off a train car in Texarkana. The airship was on its way to the world's fair in St. Louis, but it never made it.

A replica of the airship can be seen hanging from the roof of the Northeast Texas Rural Heritage Center and Museum (pittsburgtexasmuseum.com; 204 W. Marshall St., 903-856-1200). It's a funny-looking machine with fabric wings, a hydraulic system, wooden paddles, an eighty-seven-horsepower engine, and one seat.

Reverend Burrell Cannon derived his inspiration for his flying machine from the Bible. MICHAEL BARERA/FLICKR.COM

State Line Avenue
Texarkana

The message on the water tower here says, TEXARKANA IS TWICE AS NICE, but perhaps what it should say is "Texarkana Is Twice as Confusing."

State Line Avenue, which runs right through the middle of Texarkana, is just exactly what it says it is—the state line, between Texas and Arkansas.

The area code on the Texas side of the line is 903. On the Arkansas side it's 870. But it's not a long-distance call from one side of the street to the other. So if someone from the Baptist Book Store calls the Party Factory, he doesn't have to pay a long-distance fee. Not that anyone from the Baptist Book Store would have a reason to call the Party Factory.

State Line Avenue runs right up to the federal building, then goes around it. So the state line runs right through the middle of the federal building. Half

The state line runs directly through the middle of the post office in Texarkana! QUESTERMARK/FLICKR.COM

How Do You Spell That?

The name of Reklaw (population: 381), at the intersection of TX 204 and US 84, is "Walker" spelled backward. Gilbert Stafford, Reklaw's former mayor, said the town's name came about around the turn of the twentieth century. The town's original settlers were named Walker and wanted to name their town the same. But there was already a town named Walker, so they settled for spelling it in reverse.

There's a similar situation in nearby Sacul, the mayor pointed out. Sacul is "Lucas" spelled backward. The people named Lucas who settled that place ran into the same problem and came up with the same solution, Stafford said.

of the post office on the ground level is in Arkansas, and the other half is in Texas. The federal courtroom for Texas districts is on the Texas side of the building; the federal courtroom for Arkansas districts is on the Arkansas side.

When streets run across State Line Avenue, they often change names or numbers. For example, at State Line Avenue, Arkansas Boulevard changes into Texas Boulevard. So even though Texarkana has just under 38,000 people and isn't exactly what you could call huge, it's still easy to get lost there.

Arkansas has a state income tax, while Texas does not, which leads to more confusion. According to the Texarkana Chamber of Commerce, Arkansas residents who live inside the city limits of Texarkana, Arkansas, are exempt from the Arkansas income tax, regardless of where they work. Texas residents who live inside the city limits of Texarkana, Texas, and work inside the city limits of Texarkana, Arkansas, are also exempt from it. But residents of Texarkana, Texas, who work in Arkansas outside the city limits of Texarkana, Arkansas, are not exempt from the Arkansas income tax. If you can follow that, you're eligible for a desk job at H&R Block.

Of course, like every other tourist who passes through here, I got the security guard sitting in front of the federal building to take my picture by the Texarkana state line marker, which is shaped like Texas on one side and Arkansas on the other. "This will be the first time I've ever done this . . . today," said Lonnie E. Doss, the guard on duty when I stopped by on a Sunday morning.

The Draughon-Moore "Ace of Clubs" House
Texarkana

It's fortunate local lumberman and Confederate Captain James Draughon wasn't betting on pro football before he built this mansion in 1885 in the shape of a playing card. Otherwise he might have built this house to look like Texas Stadium, with an enormous hole in the roof.

Legend has it that Draughon, an early Texarkana mayor, built the floor plan in the shape of the ace of clubs because he won a large pile of money in a poker game by drawing that card.

As the literature on the mansion says of the floor plan, "Three octagonal and one long rectangular rooms are arranged around a central octagon, which serves as the rotunda of the home." The floor plan mentions a music room, a parlor, and a library, but, strangely, no pool hall. You'd think a card player would have had one.

When you walk in the front room, you are struck upside the eyeball with those black pillars decorated with gold fleurs-de-lis. The spiral staircase is incredible and is mostly freestanding.

The house, located at 420 Pine St. (texarkanamuseums.org; 903-793-4831), is part of a museum system and can be toured with a guide. Admission is $5 per person, and free for kids under three.

Hey look, it's a full house. THE LYDA HILL TEXAS COLLECTION OF PHOTOGRAPHS IN CAROL M. HIGHSMITH'S AMERICA PROJECT, LIBRARY OF CONGRESS, PRINTS AND PHOTOGRAPHS

All That We Know
Uncertain

We can be certain of one thing about the town of Uncertain (population: 94). On cypress-dotted Caddo Lake, it's certainly in a beautiful location. With its backwaters, swamps, gators, and aquatic birds, Caddo Lake looks more like your cliché vision of Louisiana than it does of what Texas is supposed to look like.

After that, details about Uncertain become, well, uncertain. The story about how this town eighteen miles northeast of Marshall on FM 2198 got its funny name is a little fuzzy.

The late historian Fred Dahmer, author of a book about the lake called *Caddo Was . . .* , was not certain how the town came to be called Uncertain.

Dahmer said he heard from friends who were on the town council at the time that the name came about because of a paperwork problem. Council members were filling out the papers to apply for township. When they came to the blank where you put in the town name, they put in the word "uncertain" because they had yet to make up their minds about what to call the place. But when the form was sent to Austin, the state capital, it was named Uncertain. So Uncertain may be Uncertain because, as Dahmer said, the former town council members "didn't know how to leave a blank."

Guided tours by boat and even paddlewheel steamboat take visitors back into the recesses of Caddo Lake for a look at the natural beauty of the region. That much is certain.

There are certainly some good reasons to visit Uncertain.

THE LYDA HILL TEXAS COLLECTION OF PHOTOGRAPHS IN CAROL M. HIGHSMITH'S AMERICA PROJECT, LIBRARY OF CONGRESS, PRINTS AND PHOTOGRAPHS

West Texas

If you want to see those miles of desert, cacti, and tumbleweeds of old Western movies, this is the place. Along I-20, giant wind turbines and oil wells dot the landscape in the Midland-Odessa area and not much else until you reach El Paso in the far western corner of the state—so far west it's in a different time zone from the rest of Texas.

Because the small towns of West Texas are so isolated, folks must have gotten so bored they created their own entertainment by collecting and displaying weird things or thinking up weird things to do. Clay Henry III, the beer-drinking goat in Lajitas, is gone now, but dozens of colorful characters are still around, providing plenty of "curiosities" to celebrate.

The part of West Texas known as the Big Bend is like nowhere else. Some folks think it's a desolate, barren landscape, but the blooming desert is amazing, and the stunning nature of the Big Bend attracts outdoor enthusiasts from around the world. Big Bend National Park encompasses three different climate zones—desert, mountains, and river. Popular activities include rafting the Rio Grande, Jeep and ATV expeditions, and hiking.

Fort Davis, Marfa, and Alpine are all worthy of a visit. Alpine is the home of Sul Ross University, the Museum of the Big Bend, and the site of the largest Cowboy Poetry Gathering in Texas, held in late February. Marfa is home to the famous Marfa Mystery Lights, a thriving contemporary arts community, and Hotel Paisano, where the classic movie Giant was filmed in 1955. Fort Davis is home to the restored Army post and McDonald Observatory, one of the world's leading astronomical research facilities. You know, the stars at night . . .

World's Largest Spring-Fed Swimming Pool
Balmorhea

Well, you just might expect to find the world's largest spring-fed swimming pool some place that gets a lot of rain, right? You probably don't expect to see it in the middle of the West Texas desert.

But that's why Balmorhea is called the "Oasis of West Texas."

The town is home to Balmorhea State Park (9207 TX 17, four miles southwest of Balmorhea in the tiny town of Toyahvale, tpwd.texas.gov/state-parks/balmorhea, 800-792-1112) and the San Solomon artesian springs, which pump out millions of gallons of cool water daily—a perfect pit stop on

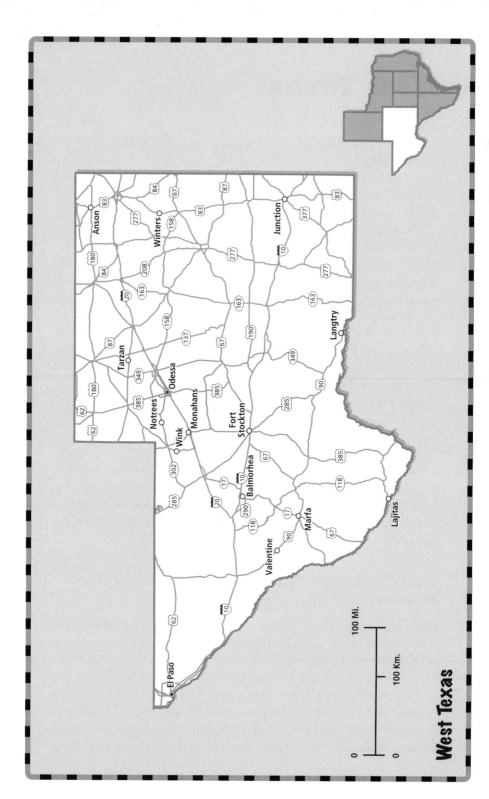

West Texas

It's not a mirage! LARS PLOUGMANN/FLICKR.COM

a desert drive. The three-quarter-acre pool boasts water that stays between 72 and 76 degrees Fahrenheit; it's so clear that swimmers share the pool with snorkelers and scuba divers who can spot native fish in the waters.

The Camino Real Hotel
El Paso

They ran a tight ship when they opened what was then called the Dream Hotel on Thanksgiving Day, 1912.

According to literature put out by the hotel, house rules included:

1. If you wet or burn your bed, you will be thrown out.
2. You are not allowed downstairs in the seating room or in the kitchen when you are drunk.
3. You must wear a shirt when you come to the seating room.

No Dancin' in Anson

The trouble with dancing is that it could lead to hanky-panky. Hence, the dancing ban on campus at Baylor University in Waco. That prohibition finally came to an end after 151 years with a street dance on April 19, 1996.

But Baylor isn't the only place in Texas that has stomped out dancing over the years. Until 1987, when a group of parents called the Footloose Club challenged a fifty-four-year-old law that banned public dances, there was no dancin' in the West Texas town of Anson. "No Dancin' in Anson" became an oft-used headline around the world. The Footloose Club parents wanted their children to be able to have their own prom. The fight got pretty ugly, with a Baptist preacher pointing out that girls could get pregnant on the dance floor.

Hey, girls could get pregnant at the laundromat, but that doesn't mean you should stop washing your clothes.

You're probably wondering at this point if the Anson ordinance was ever enforced. You bet your ballet slippers it was.

"I know at least one year the chief closed down a proposed prom," said Ricardo Ainslie, educational psychology professor at the University of Texas and the author of *No Dancin' in Anson: An American Story of Race and Social Change*. Ainslie said the chief of police showed up at the mid-1980s prom before dancing could break out. So the prom was moved to a Catholic church outside the city limits.

The Anson ordinance, passed in 1933, made dancing a $5 to $15 fine, quite a chunk of change during the Depression. The ordinance was written in such a way that you could get busted for dancing more than once in the same day. So if you were caught dancing two or three times in the same day, it could have gotten pretty expensive.

The Tiffany stained-glass dome soars above the bar at the Camino Real Hotel.

The lovely hotel is considerably looser now and even provides dirty movies on its cable television system.

Before it became a hotel, the spot (101 S. El Paso St.) was the site of a saloon operated by Ben S. Sowell, who became the first mayor of El Paso on August 15, 1873. The first official act of Sowell and his aldermen was to make it illegal to bathe in the city's drinking water supply, an acequia that ran about 150 feet north of where the hotel is today.

El Paso was a rough-and-tumble town back then. A plaque on the hotel tells about how four men were shot dead in about five seconds at this location on April 14, 1881.

The hotel itself is a jewel (camino-real.elpasobesthotels.com/en). A colorful Tiffany stained-glass dome, 25 feet in diameter, can be found in the ceiling above its large, circular bar.

The Camino Real is just six blocks from Mexico. In the old days, hotel guests gathered at the rooftop ballroom and patio—to watch the Mexican Revolution in progress across the Rio Grande.

These days, the rooftop is inaccessible to the public for liability reasons. Damned lawyers. About the only reminder of the revolution in the hotel is the Pancho Villa Room, one of the hotel's meeting rooms.

Rosa's Cantina

Every goofy guidebook ever written about Texas talks about how Marty Robbins's 1959 hit single "El Paso" was talking about this place when it mentioned Rosa's Cantina:

> Out in the West Texas town of El Paso
> I fell in love with a Mexican girl.
> Nighttime would find me in Rosa's Cantina,
> Music would play and Faleena would whirl.

Many people know the legend of how Marty Robbins supposedly was riding by Rosa's Cantina on then TX 80 on his way to Arizona when he noticed it and put the name in his song. The song stayed at numero uno for seven weeks.

I should also mention that Rosa's Cantina (3454 Doniphan Dr.; 915-833-0402) serves really cold beer at the horseshoe-shaped bar and reasonably priced Mexican food. But regardless of what the song said, the whole time I was there, there was no gal named Faleena whirling.

Former owner Roberto Zubia said he named the place Rosa's Cantina because he used to have two sisters working here—one named Trini and the other named Rosa. "So we just put cantina on the last," he said. "Who knew Marty Robbins was going to raise up and write this song about El Paso?"

Other tales offer other explanations of how the cantina got its name. Oscar and Patricia Lopez took over in 2007 and have carried on the traditions and added live music.

Rocketbuster Boots USA
El Paso

I have a couple of problems with these distinctively designed and knockout-colorful boots. First off, they're so out there that wearing them into the airport would be asking to get frisked. "You fit the profile in these boots, pal." Second, when you've got on a pair of boots that cost anywhere from $750 to $5,000, your life is ruined if you step in a puddle.

Rocketbuster Boots creates legends in leather with their custom boot designs. TEXAS TOURISM/KENNY BRAUN

But you've got to give Rocketbuster Boots an "A" for abnormality. They can make any kind of boot you want. If this isn't the only boot maker that sells a boot with the Beluga Caviar logo on it, I'd be real damned surprised.

"One banker said he wanted a show-me-the-money boot," said Nevena Christi, who owns the business with her boyfriend, Marty Snortum. They made a pair of boots out of gator that looks like $100 bills. Same color, same design. "It's called Mint Condition," Christi said of that model. Her name is on the boot. "I made myself secretary of the treasury."

They've also made boots for Sharon Stone, Steven Spielberg, Dwight Yoakam, Sylvester Stallone, Jeremy Irons, and Oprah Winfrey, among other celebrities. "We sold four pairs to Billy Bob Thornton," Christi said.

You can shop at this custom-made boot shop, at 115 South Anthony St. (rocketbuster.com; 915-541-1300), by appointment only. So don't just show up and expect to be fitted.

The colors will knock your eyes out. And they're quality boots. No cheap nails in these puppies; they use lemon-wood pegs. "They're made the oldest, hardest, most ridiculous way of boot making," Christi said.

Perhaps Rocketbuster's most spectacular accomplishment was making the world's largest real cowboy boots. The boots, decorated with Indian heads, are 5 feet tall and weigh about fifty pounds apiece. "Ours are a 328-D," Nevena said. The to-scale boots, completed on January 13, 1999, after two months of work, set a *Guinness* record for being the world's largest real custom cowboy boots.

Oh yeah, almost forgot. Nevena and Marty might not even be in the custom boot business if Marty hadn't been in a bar one night talking with a German guy. The German owned a boot company that wasn't doing so well, and Marty, a photographer, owned a Cadillac hearse he used for shoots. They traded even up, the German getting the hearse and Marty getting the boot company.

I think Marty got the better end of that deal.

Alligator Sculpture
El Paso

Why is there a monument to marshland reptiles out on the Rio Grande, where there is no marsh? Well, according to a book called *City at the Pass:*

Los Logartos by Luis Jimenez. TEXAS TOURISM/KENNY BRAUN

The First Thanksgiving

Where was the first Thanksgiving in what would eventually be known as the United States? Most ill-informed Yankees figure it was put on by those funny-hatted Pilgrims in Massachusetts. But some folks in Texas will tell you it happened in what is now far West Texas on April 28, 1598, twenty-two years before the Pilgrims hit Plymouth Rock.

Texas's version of the first Thanksgiving occurred when a group of Spaniards, led by Spanish explorer Juan de Onate, feasted on the banks of the Rio Grande after arriving near what is now El Paso. The Spaniards had just made it through a 350-mile trek from Santa Barbara, Mexico, across the Chihuahuan Desert, so they had plenty to celebrate.

In 1990, the Texas legislature passed a resolution recognizing San Elizario, Texas, on the outskirts of El Paso, as the site of the first true Thanksgiving.

An Illustrated History of El Paso, by Leon C. Metz, it's because in the 1880s, El Paso developer Fisher Satterthwaite built a fountain and pond downtown in what was then called Public Square (now called San Jacinto Plaza) and put at least two alligators in it.

Why did he do this? Maybe he had a couple of extra alligators that he didn't know what to do with. Regardless, there were alligators in the pond until 1967. Today in their place is a statue of alligators, one with his nose thrust toward the sky. The day I visited the plaza, many pigeons were sitting all over the alligators like they owned them. So sculptor Luis Jimenez created a lovely, though unusual, $50,000 pigeon perch right in the middle of downtown El Paso.

Paisano Pete,
World's (second) Largest Roadrunner
Fort Stockton

When we asked former city tour guide Billy Twowalks Kail about the town's 800-pound, 20-foot-long roadrunner statue, we learned more than we bargained for. This guy really knew his roadrunners.

"He's zygodoctile—he has two toes forward and two toes back," Kail said. "He is a member of the cuckoo family. He's one of two in the United

Although dethroned as world's largest, Pete still makes a great photo stop.
TEXAS TOURISM/ ERIK H. PRONSKE

States, the other being the rain crow. His main diet is rattlesnakes, baby quail, green lizards, and sparrows. He has an almost serpentine jaw. He swallows everything whole. He's very common to the entire Chihuahuan Desert. The word *paisano* means 'countryman.' And if you were in Italy, that would be 'friend.'"

There's more. His species name is *Geococcyx californianus*. He's called "the clown of the desert. And he doesn't fly well," Kail said. "He runs fast, flaps hard, and sails like a quail." Check him out at his location in front at East Dickinson Boulevard and Main Street.

This fellow held the title of world's largest until 2002 when New Mexico created an even larger roadrunner.

And you thought all roadrunners did was taunt Wile E. Coyote.

Deer Horn Tree
Junction

Don't lean up against this tree made out of antlers, steel-reinforcing rods, and chicken wire, unless you want a hole poked in your jeans.

Texans tend to decorate with animal parts. So when members of the Kimble (County) Business and Professional Women's Club saw a fake tree made out of deer horns in 1968 at the World's Fair in San Antonio, they figured they had to create their own version for display in town. "Some of the members came home and decided that's what we needed to do," said Frederica Wyatt, curator of the Kimble County Historical Museum (325-446-4219).

The Junction model—which you'll find in front of Kimble Processing, a deer-processing plant—stands about 15-feet high and has hundreds of sets of deer antlers, some of them with skulls still attached. Most of the horns are pretty bleached out, so the look is somewhat parched.

Wyatt isn't sure exactly how many sets of deer antlers are on the tree. Let's just say it's covered. "Oh goodness, I really have no idea," Wyatt said. "I know nobody could tell you. I don't think we've ever counted the numbers."

Don't expect to find any elk or moose snuck in there. "It's 100 percent deer," Wyatt said.

A star sits atop the tree. "We try to light it up during the Christmas season," Wyatt said. Heck, in this part of Texas even Santa is bagging Bambi when the season opens in November.

Since the tree has been around for nearly fifty years, it needs constant attention and add-ons. "You know, with time the antlers tend to deteriorate, so we have to add and replace and what have you," Wyatt said.

Junction's deer antler tree. PARIS PERMENTER AND JOHN BIGLEY

Sometimes people from other states write to complain about people in Junction going out to shoot deer for the tree, said Wyatt. But she points out that's not how it works. "Some of the deer shed their antlers," she explained. "We didn't just go out to shoot deer to get the antlers."

The Dom Rock
Out in the boondocks near Lajitas

If you visit the Dom Rock out here, watch your step. It's a long way down to the Rio Grande below.

You gotta wonder if Kevin Costner wanted to kill the location director when he found out he had to hike over a bunch of boulders out near the side of a cliff to film a key scene in his 1985 film *Fandango*.

Toward the end of the movie, which tells the story of five college buddies on their last fling before heading for Vietnam, Costner digs up a bottle of Dom Perignon champagne buried at the base of a rock, which today still has the letters "dom" scratched in the side of it. Dom, as in Dom Perignon, get it? The guys end up squirting the champagne all over each other. It's a rite of passage thing.

The view of the Rio Grande from the Dom Rock is spectacular, so if you really are fixing to waste a bottle of expensive champagne this way, this would be a great place to do it because of the scenery. Then again, maybe you should just drink it.

"It's breathtaking, it's one of the best views of the canyon," said Gina Yates of Fort Worth, who had just visited the Dom Rock the day before with her husband, Brian Curbo. People come up here to do their own version of the Costner scene. "There was a bottle, a little split of Christalino, up there. That's what most people do is take a bottle."

Unfortunately, by the time I got to the Dom Rock the next day, the bottle Gina mentioned was empty.

Part of the challenge with the Dom Rock is just finding the thing, since it's not marked on the highway and you can't see it from the road.

Here's how you get to it: Head west out of Lajitas toward Presidio on FM 170. When you get thirteen and a half miles out of town, it's on the south side of the highway at the top of the hill, out amongst all those rocks overlooking the river. Park in the pullover on the south side of the road, across from the sign that says HILL. USE LOW GEAR. Hike about 100 feet toward the Rio Grande, and you're there. Be careful, though. It's a long way down to the river. Running shoes or hiking boots are recommended.

Oh, by the way: you might want to buy your Dom Perignon before you get to Lajitas, since it's in the middle of nowhere and about five hundred miles from Austin.

The Jersey Lilly Saloon
Langtry

Don't get any wild ideas about finding a beer in this place.

From 1882 until his death in 1903, Judge Roy Bean served both justice and drinks out of this bar, halfway between nowhere and too-late-to-turn-back. Judge Bean was the law "west of the Pecos." Bean held court in the saloon or on the front steps.

These days the bare wooden building is run as a tourist attraction by the Texas Department of Transportation, which has a comfortable air-conditioned visitor center in front of the old saloon building.

Actually, you can learn quite a bit about Judge Bean at the alleged saloon by reading the historical marker and listening to the sound blurb that

Today the old saloon serves maps and travel advice.

plays when you push the red button. When the transcontinental railroad came through this part of West Texas, the Texas Rangers needed someone to corral the drunks. So they made Judge Bean justice of the peace. The closest courthouse was 125 miles away in Fort Stockton.

"He basically fined the drunks and kept the money," said Ginger Harrell, a travel counselor who used to work in the visitor center. "He hung no one. The movies have distorted the facts tremendously. He never hung anybody or killed anybody."

Because there was no jail here, Bean fined the drunks and pocketed the fines. That seems a little unfair, doesn't it? Here's a guy serving drinks in the desert, then busting people for getting gassed. What a setup.

Incidentally, the saloon was named for English actress Lillie Langtry, who Bean admired and for whom he named the town.

The Marfa Lights
Marfa

Who knows what causes these mysterious lights that come on and off in the distance? Whatever it is, the city makes hay out of it. About ten miles east of Marfa on US 90, you'll come to the mystery lights viewing area, a rest stop where you can pull over and look for the lights.

MARFA'S MYSTERY LIGHTS VIEWING AREA, the sign says. NIGHT TIME ONLY. Did they really need to put that notice on the sign? What kind of idiot would go look for lights in the sky during daylight?

Lineaus Lorette of Fort Davis and I went to see the Marfa Lights on a Saturday night in July. When we got there, the viewing area was packed. Dogs were barking and people were yakking. Some folks were looking at what they were pretty darned sure were the Marfa Lights. Just above the horizon, miles away, round white lights would come on, one at a time. Then they would burn out. Then they would come back on for a while. Then they would disappear again. They'd pop up in various spots.

Marfa's rugged landscape holds mysteries. TEXAS TOURISM/KENNY BRAUN

There are several theories as to what causes the Marfa Lights, which some say come in various colors and sometimes move around. Sightings have been recorded since 1883. Apaches believed the lights were stars dropping to the earth. Lineaus believes they are probably a reflection of the stars below the horizon, bouncing off the atmosphere.

Me? I think there's a guy off in the distance showing his vacation slides from Hawaii.

But whatever they are, Marfa (visitmarfa.com) plays them up. SEE MYSTERY LIGHTS, said the banner on a motel in Marfa. On Labor Day, Marfa has a Marfa Lights celebration with a parade (marfatxlights.com).

Tourists come from all over to see the lights. The late Pancho Borunda who owned a Marfa restaurant once said "Everybody's seen something different. In fact, we had some guys in here last night who had come all the way from Houston. They were asking questions like, 'When's the best time to see 'em, and should we bring some beer out there?'"

The answers to those two questions are (1) after dark and (2) yes.

Prada Marfa
Marfa

Marfa, in far West Texas, is a community of folks who march to distinctly different drummers, and nobody cares. Maybe those "mystery lights" have something to do with it. Anyway, Prada Marfa is defined by its creators as "a pop architectural land art project." Most folks define it as "What the hell is that?" It sits in the middle of nowhere, about a mile and a half northwest of Valentine, which is about thirty-five miles northwest of Marfa on US 90.

The sculptors, Michael Elmgreen, a Dane, and Ingar Dragset, a Norwegian, who now live in Germany, are acclaimed for their works of wit, whimsy, and sometime subversive looks at the cultural world around them. Many think Prada Marfa is a surrealist commentary on Western materialism.

Miuccia Prada herself was consulted, personally chose the pseudo-store's merchandise, and gave permission to use the Prada logo. Built at a cost of $80,000 and opened October 1, 2005, it's made of biodegradable adobe that will slowly melt back into the landscape. So designed to never need repairs, the masterminds probably never heard of vandals. In three days, all the handbags and shoes were stolen and the walls decorated with graffiti.

Repaired and restocked, the new store is a booby trap for thieves. The walls and windows are stronger, the shoes fit right feet only, and the purses have no bottoms, hiding part of the security system. In a place known for

Only one question: Why? TEXAS TOURISM/KENNY BRAUN.

"bizarreness," this may be one of the most bizarre. And thousands of visitors each year visit the fake store in the middle of nowhere.

Now That's a Lot of Concrete
Monahans

If you like to plan your vacation around places where you can look at enormous amounts of concrete, this is your town.

The Million Barrel Museum (400 Museum Blvd.; 432-943-8401) is primarily an ill-fated ugly huge concrete tank built by Shell in 1928 to store oil. In the late 1950s, they filled it with water and tried stocking it with trout. The trout died. So what happened to the trout? "I would say it was a lack of vegetation and circulating water," said Lee Nichols, the museum's curator, caretaker, and maintenance man.

Shell built this semi-bowl-shaped monstrosity—the floor alone is large enough to hold five football fields, Nichols said—to store oil because at the time it didn't have enough pipelines to distribute the oil. And this booger went up fast.

"A tent city grew up around it," Nichols said. "It was like an army of men. They worked twenty-four hours a day. That's why it only took ninety days to build."

Wonder if they can see this thing from space!
THE LYDA HILL TEXAS COLLECTION OF PHOTOGRAPHS IN CAROL M. HIGHSMITH'S AMERICA PROJECT,
LIBRARY OF CONGRESS, PRINTS AND PHOTOGRAPHS DIVISION

Maybe if they'd taken a little more time to build the tank it wouldn't have started leaking oil so fast. But what really killed the tank as an oil-storage unit, Nichols said, was the stock market crash of 1929. The price of oil dropped from $1.75 a barrel to a nickel or a dime, he said. So keeping oil around didn't seem quite so important.

So the tank sat there gray and empty until the 1950s, when an entrepreneur named Wayne Long bought the thing, at first with the intention of racing cars in it. "I had an old gentleman come in here, and he's one of the guys who raced in there, and he said they did that three weekends in a row," Nichols said.

The concrete surface was too bumpy for stock cars, though. "It was tearing up their cars, so they stopped," Nichols said.

In 1958, the tank was used as a water park—for one day. Melody Park, named for Long's dog, opened and closed on October 5, 1958. "Here's a picture of the only boat and ski show that ever took place there, in 1958," Nichols said. "I was an eyewitness to that. I was only eight years old."

The tank had other uses. "In the early fifties they used to square-dance in the tank," Nichols said. "There would be about 150 [people] that would show up on Friday nights. Some of our museum board members did that and remember that." He said Anita Pigman, a member of the museum board, still "vividly remembers" square-dancing in the tank.

Nichols said that in the 1970s some crazy local guys tried to blow up the tank with a bomb, which explains some of the ruts in the floor. "They ended up in wheelchairs from doing drugs; that's the kind of guys they were," Nichols said.

These days the tank, which has an amphitheater on one end, is used for a variety of functions, including high school reunions and concerts. And the local high school kids scribble on the concrete walls—you know, stuff like "Natalie 'n' Gene."

To Be or Not to Be
Odessa

Odessa College is the site of one of only three re-creations of Shakespeare's theater in the world.

The late Anthony Ridley, the theater's artistic director until 2012, once pointed out, "There are some striking differences, of course, one of them being there's a roof on it. The other big difference is we have seats in the Globe. Our seating area would be the big old cockpit where the lower classes called the groundlings would stand and watch the plays." So today's groundlings—maybe the oil field roughnecks—can sit in comfort in this Globe in red plush upholstered chairs.

This is not to say that the theater doesn't have some local touches. Ann Wilson, the theater's manager, who knows every nook and cranny of this theater, pronounces it "thee-A-ter," which is how you're supposed to say it out in West Texas, regardless of what King Lear might think.

The idea for this theater popped up, Wilson said, when the late Marjorie Morris, a high school English teacher at the time, gave her students an assignment to build models of Shakespeare's Globe. "When one of her students turned his in, he said, 'Wouldn't it be neat to have a Globe Theatre right here in Odessa?'" Wilson said.

The theater comes with a re-creation of Anne Hathaway's cottage next door. Wilson said they had to affix the heavy wooden block that serves as the oven door to the wall for safety purposes. "When they were building it, there was this woman who decided to bake something to see what it was like to bake back then, and she dropped the wooden block on her foot," Wilson explained.

All the world's a stage…even West Texas. PARIS PERMENTER AND JOHN BIGLEY

Anne Hathaway's cottage doesn't have a thatched roof for a couple of reasons. For one, the fire marshal wouldn't allow it because of the fire hazard that would create in this dry desert climate.

Then there was the expense of the thatch. "When they were doing it, they found out they don't grow that kind of material here, and the expense in importing that kind of grass would be astronomical," Wilson said.

On the other hand, just like in Shakespeare's Globe, this theater has three Old English–style turrets up above the stage known as "the heavens." In Shakespeare's day, characters coming out of "the heavens" were lowered down to the stage by cable.

"We haven't done that because it's kinda dangerous," Wilson said. And characters rising from hell—like the "double, double toil, and trouble" witches from *Macbeth*—reach the stage by coming up through a trap door. Little boys touring the theater love visiting the room that represents hell below the trap door. "They like to go down through the trap door that goes into hell, then come up," Wilson said.

People come from hundreds of miles away to attend plays here. Of course, way out here it's hundreds of miles away to a lot of places. "In the summer, people traveling will stop here in Odessa just to see the Globe," Wilson said. "A couple of times we've had a reporter from London come to do a story on the Globe."

The guy from London was probably impressed that once a month this Globe features a show of country or gospel music, or a combination of the two. Haggard and Hamlet: no place but Texas.

For more information, punch up globesw.org or call (432) 335-6818.

It's a Bird, It's a Plane, It's a Really Large Hunk of Iron
Odessa

Out here in the West Texas desert is a great place for a meteorite to land because it ain't going to get much uglier even after something big hits it. Except for the pump jacks and the scrub brush, there isn't much to look at in the oil patch.

Of course, there was even less going on 63,500 years ago when a 250-ton hunk of mostly iron slammed into the ground at seven miles a second. That's 25,200 miles an hour.

The Odessa Meteor Crater, 500-feet or so in diameter, was about 100-feet deep at the time of impact. But at its current depth of about twelve feet, this crater, the second largest meteor crater in the United States, isn't nearly as impressive as it was in its youth.

"After the explosion, about fifteen feet of rubble that had blown up in the air fell back in the crater," said Tom Rodman, the attorney and oil and gas man who served as president of the nonprofit organization that developed the Odessa Meteor Crater Museum southwest of town on I-20, exit 108, and south two miles on Meteor Crater Road (netwest.com/virtdomains/meteorcrater/About.htm; 432-381-0946). "Then the sand started blowing, and it filled up."

The crater is shallow enough that you can take a walking tour through it without worrying about busting your butt. On the other hand, there is a sign at the beginning of the tour that tells you to watch out for snakes.

This is not to say the crater couldn't have been a lot worse, what with all that space junk flying around out there. "If an asteroid the size of Rhode Island hit, it would be the end of the world," Rodman pointed out.

While you're waiting for that to happen, there is plenty to see in the museum, although you could go through the whole thing (maybe we should say the hole thing) in an hour. You can see various chunks of the actual Odessa meteorite, although they aren't exactly sexy in color, since the Odessa meteorite was 90 percent iron.

"On the outside they're pure brown because they're rust," Rodman pointed out. In a way, that's good because that means the meteor chunks

It came from outer space, really ODESSA CONVENTION & VISITORS BUREAU

don't clash with the area's ubiquitous oil field equipment. On the other hand, if you cut into the same chunks, they're shiny and metallic on the inside.

They're also heavy. In the mid 1970s somebody stole the largest specimen from the Odessa meteor—a 105-pound chunk—from the society's earlier museum. And the thieves wouldn't have needed a truck to do it. "A 105-pound meteorite is no bigger than a basketball," Rodman said.

So how did Rodman get interested in meteorites? "Back in 1963 my father owned a ranch that surrounded the meteor crater," he explained. "Our rancher caught a trespasser out there digging up meteorites. So he was arrested for trespassing. Turned out he had about 300 pounds of Odessa meteorites he had dug up."

So what do you do with Odessa meteor chunks? "Sell 'em. They've always been very valuable." Rodman said the stuff will sell for over $100 a pound as collector's items.

Speaking of collecting, Rodman is such a meteor buff that he even has a collection of meteor movie videotapes in a box. His favorite is a film I'd never heard of called, simply, *Meteorites!* "It didn't make a big splash," he said.

Notrees

Oh, yes there are. So this town of about twenty people is inappropriately named. Although just barely. 'Cause there aren't a lot of trees out here, about twenty miles west of Odessa. The trees in Notrees are kind of droopy looking.

"There's a few elm, and some people have planted some pine trees now," said Jannifer Whitehead, postmaster of the Notrees Post Office. Notrees also has an oil company and a volunteer fire department.

Whitehead said Charles Brown named the town in 1946, after moving here with his family. "He wanted to name the town Judy, for his third daughter," Whitehead said. "But when he sent the name to Austin, they wrote back there was already a town named Judy. So he was looking out the window and noticed there were no trees. So he decided to name the town Notrees."

World's Largest Jackrabbit (Jack Ben Rabbit)
Odessa

The best part of this big-eared, 8-foot-tall fiberglass statue, located at 8th Street and North Sam Houston Avenue, is the jackrabbit recipe on the back of one of the two plaques next to it:

First, catch your rabbit. Dress rabbit. Salt and soak in brine, then boil 'til tender. Add pepper to taste. Fill pot with dumplings. Cook 'til dough is done.

It's recipes like these that explain why Kentucky Fried Chicken was invented.

One marker tells about how jackrabbits can do forty-five miles an hour, and that they were a "prized" source of food among the Indians. Hey, if you were a prized food among the Indians, you could do forty-five miles an hour, too.

The other marker addresses the 1932 Odessa Rodeo's world's first championship jackrabbit roping. The alleged event was allegedly won by Grace Hendricks, who beat out several male competitors by allegedly roping

It's okay to pose with Jack for photos, just don't try roping him.
ODESSA CONVENTION & VISITORS BUREAU

a jackrabbit from horseback in five seconds flat. I'd have to see a video of that before I put much stock in it.

Incidentally, the World's Largest Jackrabbit, as it has been billed, now has offspring—thirty-six additional jackrabbit statues that went up all over town in April 2004 through February 2005.

"We called it Jackrabbit Jamboree," said Pat Owsley, formerly of the Odessa Convention and Visitors Bureau. "We solicited artists in the Permian

Basin area to submit their concept of what they would do for a rabbit. We had a juried show where people selected the ones that they liked."

Among the other rabbits commissioned were *Jacks Are Wild* (a rabbit covered with playing cards), *Hare on a Hog* (a rabbit in biker attire, including goggles), and *Gusher the Hare* (a rabbit sporting a drawing of an oil well). So I guess you could say the jackrabbits were multiplying like rabbits around here.

Odessa Stonehenge
Odessa

Yes, Texas is home to not one but two Stonehenge replicas. Like its cousin in Ingram, the Odessa Stonehenge, located on Preston Smith Road, is smaller than its British counterpart—but not by much.

Located on the campus of The University of Texas of the Permian Basin, this rocky replica took just six weeks to construct (compared to 2,000 years for the ancient model). The twenty stone blocks are just like the original in terms of shape. The circle is as large as its ancient counterpart but slightly shorter.

Make no mistake about it, though, these are definitely Texas-sized stones. Each of the limestone blocks weighs over 20,000 pounds.

Students in physics, math, and geology have made pilgrimages to Odessa's Stonehenge. ODESSA CONVENTION & VISITORS BUREAU

Valentine's Day

Thanks to the town's name, this place is transformed into a veritable Cupid City in mid-February each year.

Every year, the two-woman post office in this town of 187 gets about 20,000 Valentine cards from hither and yon. The record was in 1994 when over 39,000 cards from around the world came in to receive the Valentine's postmark.

To make it even more special, each year this post office, nicknamed "the Love Station of Texas," uses a different cancellation stamp. The stamp is selected from artwork submitted by Valentine students in grades 7-12.

To get your Valentine's card stamped from Valentine, Texas, here's what you do, according to 2017 info from the United States Postal Service:

1. Buy a Valentine's Day card and address it to your sweetie just as you would if you were mailing it yourself.

2. Place a First-Class Mail postage stamp on that Valentine's Day card.

3. Get a slightly larger envelope and place the addressed, stamped Valentine's card inside that larger envelope. Seal the envelope.

4. Address that larger envelope to:

   Valentine's Day Postmark
   Postmaster
   311 W California Ave.
   Valentine, TX 79854-9998

5. Stamp the larger envelope with appropriate postage and mail it.

Starting two weeks before Valentine's Day, the post office will open the outer envelope and hand stamp the inner envelope, shipping it and your Valentine's wishes...along with that very special Valentine, Texas, postmark...off to your significant watchamacallit.

It's a Jungle Out There

How did Tarzan, a ranching and farming community in a flat place, get its name?

According to information available at the little Tarzan post office, the town was founded in 1924 by Tant Lindsay, who later submitted a list of six names for the town. All of the names were rejected by the Post Office Department in Washington because they were already being used in Texas. Lindsay submitted four more lists, all of them turned down for the same reason.

So for the sixth list, Lindsay sent in six names from the Edgar Rice Burroughs book *Tarzan, Lord of the Jungle,* which he had just bought for his daughter. The names were Lord, Jungle, Edgar, Rice, Burroughs—and Tarzan.

Washington approved Tarzan.

The Roy Orbison Museum
Wink

If you wink going through Wink, you'll miss the Roy Orbison Museum on TX 115 (213 E Hendricks Blvd.; 915-527-3622). And that would be a shame, because you wouldn't get to try on the late singer's famous prescription sunglasses.

Roy Orbison, he of "Oh, Pretty Woman" fame, may have had a uniquely haunting voice, but his eyes apparently weren't much. If you have average eyes, when you look through his prescription sunglasses, it's kind of like opening your eyes underwater.

The sunglasses were donated to the museum by Orbison's widow, Barbara Orbison. Museum staff will take a photo of you wearing these glasses if you wish. Then, they'll ask you to autograph it, and they'll tack it to the wall. So the one-room museum has a bunch of goofy-looking photos of people wearing Roy Orbison's sunglasses.

Roy Orbison grew up in Wink and graduated from high school here in 1954. At the museum you can see all manner of Roy Orbison memorabilia,

The man with the big voice came from a small Texas town. ROBERT BROWN

including records, photos, high school yearbooks, and a poster from a 1968 movie Orbison starred in, *The Fastest Guitar Alive*.

"Doomed effort to turn recording star Orbison into a movie star—with the dumbest title imaginable for a Civil War espionage story!" reads the review of this movie from Leonard Maltin's 1998 *Movie & Video Guide*.

They even have a traffic sign sent to the museum from Branson, Missouri. TOW AWAY ZONE—ORBISON FANS PARKING ONLY, the sign says.

Each year the museum holds a Roy Orbison Festival on the weekend closest to Orbison's birthday (April 23) in his birthplace of Vernon, Texas. So guess what they call the festival's beauty pageant? The Pretty Woman Pageant. What else could they possibly call it?

If you're interested in seeing the museum, call Wink City Hall at (432) 527-3441. It's by appointment only.

Frigid Fight Song

In many places in Texas, we figure it's a cold day if the dog's water bowl freezes an eighth of an inch on the back porch. We know chili better than chilly, if you catch my drift.

But because of the town name, in Winters they play the cold theme up big. The high school band uses the mellow "Walkin' in a Winter Wonderland" as the school's fight song. A song popularized by Guy Lombardo and his Royal Canadians, and it ends up in a Texas fight song?

Actually, the fight part of the song is buried in the middle of the tune. "The song starts out, *bump bah bah, dah dah dah dah*, real upbeat," said Winters High band director Phillip Mooney. "But about halfway through it goes into an actual fight song."

Winters High, he pointed out, is the home of the fightin' Blizzards. What else?

Even though you wouldn't think people would get real fired up with a song that starts out "Sleighbells ring, are you listenin'?" the song has been used for quite some time at football games here. "I think I heard a recording of the band playing it in the late 1940s, and it's pretty much unchanged," Mooney said.

Winters High uses other wintry themes. "Back in the 1960s they had a little jazz band called the Snowmen, and they have the Glacier King and Queen," Mooney said.

What they don't have is a ski area. And most of the ice comes in a plastic bag. Despite the name, this ain't Colorado.

The town name has nothing to do with the climate. According to *The New Handbook of Texas*, Winters is named for John N. Winters, a rancher and land agent who donated land for the first school.

The Wink Sinks
Near Wink

Used to be there was only one Wink Sink, a big hole in the ground off CR 205 that appeared mysteriously almost overnight in the oil fields between Kermit and Wink in 1980. But now there are two Wink Sinks—thanks to a second large hole discovered in the ground in May of 2002 about a half mile southeast of the original Wink Sink.

This is a good part of the world for large holes to appear, since it's so flat, making them easy to find. Besides, not many people live out this way, so it's less likely for somebody to be standing over a large hole when it decides to show up.

Not that you could miss these holes. The first Wink Sink is no slouch in the size department—now measuring more than 400 feet across and 80 feet deep (and it keeps growing). But it's no match for the new crater, which is even more humongous, spanning up to 900 feet at its widest point

The sinks are barely visible from the highway and that's as close as you're permitted to go to these unusual formations that continue to grow in size. Some scientists speculate that more holes will develop, or the two existing sinks might someday collapse into one.

So next time you blink, there might be a third Wink Sink—or one giant one.

In Wink, it pays to watch out where you step. GANITOID/CC-BY-SA-3.0

High Plains

The landscape of the High Plains (aka the Panhandle) is mostly flat, except for the breathtaking canyon lands of Palo Duro Canyon. The legacy of the Old West is evident throughout this area dominated by ranching, agriculture, and oil.

Amarillo is one of the two main cities in the Panhandle. A stretch of historic Route 66 runs through town, drawing a legion of tourists and history buffs. About fifteen miles south of Amarillo, the town of Canyon is the "Gateway to Palo Duro Canyon" and home of the Panhandle Plains Historical Museum (panhandleplains.org), considered by many to be the best natural history museum in Texas. Driving along the flat grasslands, it's quite a surprise when it abruptly breaks and reveals the vast chasm of Palo Duro Canyon. At more than 20,000 acres, the rugged beauty of Palo Duro Canyon State Park offers great hiking, mountain biking, and horseback riding.

Farther south, you enter the Llano Estacado, one of the largest flatland areas in the world, where you'll find Lubbock, birthplace and home of the late Buddy Holly. The home of Texas Tech University, Lubbock offers all the attractions of a big city with cultural venues, good restaurants, and excellent museums. Two outstanding ones are the thirty-acre Ranching Heritage Center and Silent Wings, a museum dedicated to the glider pilots of World War II. In addition, several award-winning wineries cluster around Lubbock.

Music festivals are huge events in the High Plains, an area that has produced an inordinate number of singers and musicians, from Bob Wills, "King of Western Swing," to Buddy Holly, Mac Davis, Waylon Jennings, Larry Gatlin, Jimmy Dean, Earnest Tubb, and Tanya Tucker, among others.

The Big Texan Steak Ranch
Amarillo

If you've ever had a hankering to consume a piece of meat the size of a double-wide, this is the restaurant for you.

If you can finish off the 72-ounce top sirloin in an hour or less, it's yours for free—if you can also down the baked potato, shrimp cocktail, dinner roll, and salad that come with it. If not, it'll cost you $72.

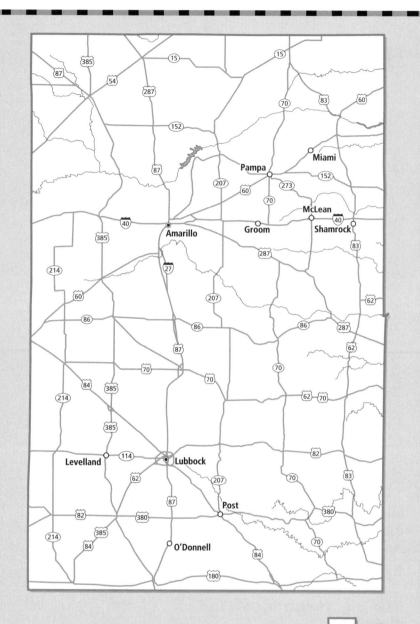

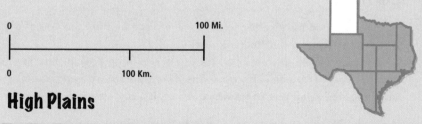

High Plains

So what is it that gets them? "It's the croutons," joked Bobby Lee, one of the owners of this restaurant off I-40's exit 75 (bigtexan.com; 806-372-6000).

Since the challenge began in 1962 (at a price of $9.95), over 61,000 people have tried to complete the meal, and just 9,300 of them have been successful. (The exact number is a mystery because the pre-1991 records were destroyed.) "It's about the size of a catcher's mitt," Lee said of the steak.

Not everyone who has accomplished the task has been a hulk. Lee said a 95-pound reporter from the *Wall Street Journal* ate the whole thing. But he didn't say if that weight was before or after. In the summer of 2009, a seventy-year-old man displaced a sixty-nine-year-old grandmother as the oldest person to eat the whole thing. The youngest was an eleven-year-old boy who asked for dessert afterward.

The fastest time ever was turned in by former Cincinnati Reds pitcher Frank Pastore, who finished up in under ten minutes in 1984. Too bad the game of baseball doesn't move that fast.

To get a steak for free here, you have to finish every last bite within an hour.
TEXAS TOURISM/KENNY BRAUN

Danny Lee, Bobby's brother and an owner, said every once in a while someone will make practical use of the steak deal. He said one guy who ordered it was taking his sweet time eating it, but ordered a dozen extra rolls. "He said, 'I'm going all the way to California, and I wanted to make some sandwiches,'" Danny recalled.

It hasn't been all fun and games at the Big Texan Steak Ranch, though. In October of 2003, George, the restaurant's 8½-pound pet rattler, got loose from his cage in the gift shop. This presented a thrill for management, because the restaurant was open at the time and they really didn't want George crawling up some tourist's leg.

"There was a pretty good crowd. Thank God we found it," Bobby Lee said. "We found it in about twenty minutes. That was the longest twenty minutes of my life."

Then, in 1998, there was the escaped convict from Indiana who shot himself to death in Room 223 of the restaurant's motel after the police came and surrounded the place. "It was a big deal; they brought a SWAT team out and everything," Bobby Lee recalled. Ever since that event, he claimed, there has been "weird stuff going on in that room."

And speaking of the hotel, if your ride happens to have four legs, have no worries: Big Texan has its own Horse Hotel.

Poetry in Motion
Near Amarillo

If you're in the mood to be put on, you can't miss this one, south of Amarillo.

"I met a traveler from an antique land / Who said: Two vast and trunkless legs of stone / Stand in the desert," reads the poem "Ozymandias," by the immortal English poet Percy Bysshe Shelley.

So just to tweak everybody's nose, the wild and wacky Stanley Marsh 3 (now deceased) commissioned Amarillo sculptor Lightnin' McDuff to build two large, trunkless legs of concrete reinforced with steel: one 24 feet high and the other 34 feet high. The legs get a lot of attention. "People go out there sometimes and paint his toenails," Marsh said. "And I understand there have been three marriages out there."

The legs may not be standing in the desert, exactly, but they are standing behind a barbed-wire fence all by themselves in a pasture off I-27 at Sundown Lane, south of Amarillo. You can't miss them. They're the only big concrete legs with large feet out there.

The work, like the poem, is called *Ozymandias*. Why did Marsh pick this poem? "It's a poem about the futility of building monuments, so, of course, I built a monument to it," he once explained.

The legs come with a phony Texas historical marker Marsh concocted to further muddy the waters. The marker says that Shelley penned his poem at this location in 1819 when he and his wife, Mary Wollstonecraft Shelley, the author of *Frankenstein*, "came across these ruins" while they were "on their horseback trek over the great plains of New Spain."

Almost everything on this marker is complete and utter horse doots. My favorite part is the paragraph at the bottom of the marker that explains why the legs have no face: "The visage (or face) was damaged by students from Lubbock after losing to Amarillo in competition." The marker goes on to say that the face will be replaced, and if you want to see the original, you can find it at the Amarillo Museum of Natural History.

There is no Amarillo Museum of Natural History. But people called all the time, trying to find it.

Incidentally, unknown pranksters painted gym socks on the legs. Marsh didn't do the work, but since he liked it, he took credit for it.

If you build it, they will come. AMBOO WHO?/FLICKR.COM

Helium Columns Monument
Amarillo

The Helium Time Columns Monument and Museum, located in Amarillo just outside the Don Harrington Discovery Center (discoverycenteramarillo.org; 1200 Streit Dr., 806-355-9547), definitely ranks as an unusual Texas sight. The four columns are filled with books and memorabilia about life in 1968.

Why 1968? Why, that was the 100th anniversary of when helium was discovered. I thought everybody knew that.

To make things a little more unusual, the books are sealed in a helium-filled atmosphere, one that's not to be opened until the year 2550. So, you've got plenty of time to make your plans to attend that event.

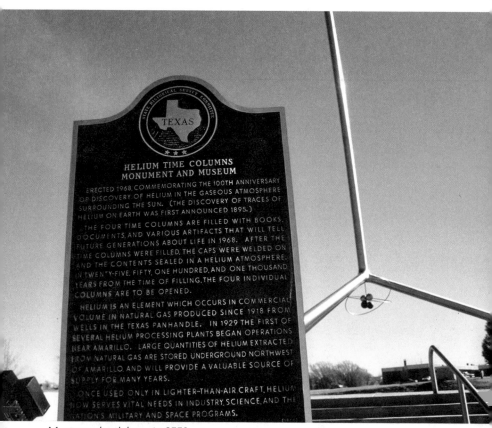

Meet you back here in 2550. PARIS PERMENTER AND JOHN BIGLEY

Cadillac Ranch
Near Amarillo

Bankrolled by the late eccentric millionaire Stanley Marsh 3, this ranch in a field next to I-40 on Frontage Road is where ten vintage Cadillacs are buried nose down in the ground with their tail fins thrust toward the sky. Established to outline the history of changes to the Cadillac tail fin, the display is the Panhandle's answer to the Statue of Liberty. It's what you go look at when you're up this way.

"You can't drive by it when there's not somebody out there," said Jackie Anderson, who worked for Marsh's investment company. "And there'll be Germans or Japanese, tourists from all over the world."

In 1998, the Caddies were decorated for the holiday season. "We just painted 'em like Christmas trees," Anderson said. "Green, with tinsel and ornaments and all kinds of stuff." Years of visitors have added their own contributions to the Caddy sculptures which are now covered with a mishmash of graffiti.

Check out the Cadillac Ranch, a line of ten Caddies buried in a dirt field.
PARIS PERMENTER AND JOHN BIGLEY

Texas-Sized Claims

It's no secret that Texans like to brag about their state. That boastfulness is apparent when you consider all the places in the state that claim to be the biggest, the best, or the capital of this or that. Here's a partial (more-or-less official) list of state superlatives:

Anahuac: Alligator Capital of Texas

Baird: Antique Capital of Texas

Breckenridge: Mural Capital of Texas

Brownsville: Chess Capital of Texas

Buda: Outdoor Capital of Texas

Caldwell: Kolache Capital of Texas

Clifton: Norwegian Capital of Texas

Commerce: Bois d'arc Capital of Texas

Danevang: Danish Capital of Texas

Denton: Redbud Capital of Texas

Dublin: Irish Capital of Texas

Electra: Pump Jack Capital of Texas

Elgin: Sausage Capital of Texas

Floresville: Peanut Capital of Texas

Fredericksburg: Polka Capital of Texas

Friona: Cheeseburger Capital of Texas

Gatesville: Spur Capital of Texas

George West: Storyfest Capital of Texas

Georgetown: Red Poppy Capital of Texas

Glen Rose: Dinosaur Capital of Texas

Hamilton: Dove Capital of Texas

Hawkins: Pancake Capital of Texas

Hearne: Sunflower Capital of Texas

Hutto: Hippo Capital of Texas

Jasper: Butterfly Capital of Texas

Jefferson: Bed and Breakfast Capital of Texas

Knox City: Seedless Watermelon Capital of Texas

Llano: Deer Capital of Texas

Lockhart: Barbecue Capital of Texas

Longview: Purple Martin Capital of Texas

Marlin: Hot Mineral Water Capital of Texas

Mauriceville: Crawfish Capital of Texas

McCarney: Wind Energy Capital of Texas

Mesquite: Rodeo Capital of Texas

Midland: Ostrich Capital of Texas

Midlothian: Cement and Steel Capital of Texas

Mount Pleasant: Bass Capital of Texas

Navasota: Blues Capital of Texas

Odessa: Jackrabbit Capital of Texas

Palacios: Shrimp Capital of Texas

Plano: Hot Air Balloon Capital of Texas

Sanderson: Cactus Capital of Texas

West: Czech Heritage Capital of Texas

West Tawokoni: Catfish Capital of Texas

And We'll Top That: World-Sized Claims

Anthony: Leap Year Capital of the World

Athens: Blackeyed Pea Capital of the World

Austin: Live Music Capital of the World

Bandera: Cowboy Capital of the World

Corsicana: Fruit Cake Capital of the World

Crystal City: Spinach Capital of the World

Cuero: Turkey Capital of the World

Denison: Wine Root Stock Capital of the World

Jacksonville: Tomato Capital of the World

Kenedy: Texas Horned Lizard Capital of the World

McAllen: Square Dance Capital of the World

Naples: Watermelon Capital of the World

San Angelo: Wool and Mohair Capital of the World

Seguin: Pecan Capital of the World

Terlingua: Chili Capital of the World

Turkey: Western Swing Capital of the World

Tyler: Rose Capital of the World

Weatherford: Cutting Horse Capital of the World

Really Big Cross
Groom

"I just wanted to advertise for our Creator in a bold manner. That's about as bold as you can get," said Steve Thomas, a structural engineer from Pampa.

No kidding. The 190-foot-tall steel cross Thomas put up in 1995 on the south side of I-40 at exit 112 (crossministries.net; 806-248-9006) is so big that you can see it up to twenty miles away. This cross, lit up at night, was billed as the largest cross in the Western Hemisphere, until a 198-foot steel cross at I-57 and I-70 at Effingham, Illinois, was completed in 2001.

"There's one other cross larger and that's in Spain," Thomas said, speaking of a 500-foot-tall masonry cross sixty miles north of Madrid, built by Francisco Franco. Being a dictator, Franco probably didn't have to use his own money. Thomas, however, spent $500,000 to build this cross.

This is not just a cross. It is a cross complex with a big parking lot that will accommodate eighteen-wheelers, the stations of the cross done in bronze, even a gift shop with indoor plumbing.

"We get 1,000 or 2,000 [people] a day stopping, and 10 million a year go by," said Thomas, head of an outfit called Cross of Our Lord Jesus Christ Ministries. He said he put up the cross to combat "X-rated stuff, period, not just on the highways," as well as alcohol and gambling. In other words the cross is lit up at night in hopes of keeping people from getting lit up at night.

You can't miss the second-largest cross in the Western Hemisphere. It's 190 feet tall. THE LYDA HILL TEXAS COLLECTION OF PHOTOGRAPHS IN CAROL M. HIGHSMITH'S AMERICA PROJECT, LIBRARY OF CONGRESS, PRINTS AND PHOTOGRAPHS DIVISION

What's Your Major?

Okay, kids, no fair looking at each others' work. Here are some of the questions on this semester's country-and-western music final:

1. True or false. George Jones was loaded when he hit that bridge.

2. Fill in the blanks: Let's go to Luckenbach, Texas, with____, _____, and the ____.

3. What doesn't fit in this grouping: trains, mamma, gettin' drunk, pickup trucks, TGI Friday's?

Actually, I just made those questions up. But you really can get an associate of applied arts degree in country-and-western music from South Plains College, a junior college in Levelland (spccreativearts.com; 806-894-9611). Because it's both country and western music, I guess that would make it a double major. Either way, South Plains College was the first college in Texas to offer a degree plan specifically for country-and-western music, said John Hartin, retired chairman of the creative arts department and a country music performer himself. Hartin founded the program in 1975.

"The students who leave here are fully equipped to go out and compete in the music business, whether it be as a performer, sound engineer, or the camera part of it," said Tammy Amos, department secretary. I wonder if that means they teach them how to ride cross-country on a Greyhound bus.

Seriously, the program has three full recording studios—among them the Tom T. Hall Recording Studio and the Waylon Jennings Recording Studio. Students can take private lessons on a variety of instruments, from mandolin to upright bass.

The school's alumni include Lee Ann Womack, Natalie Maines of the Dixie Chicks, Heath Wright of Ricochet, and Ricky Turpin, fiddle player with Asleep at the Wheel, among others.

The "Leaning Tower of Groom," is a tilted water tower that used to advertise a now-extinct truck stop off old U.S. Route 66 in tiny Groom.

Leaning Water Tower
Groom

Your eyes are not playing tricks on you.

The water tower is leaning. And, no, it is not leaning due to fracking, an earthquake, a Panhandle windstorm, or even Texas's melting heat.

Ralph Britten once purchased the water tower and had it installed at this site as a promotional gimmick for his now-defunct truck stop. The truck stop is no longer there but the leaning tower remains a popular photo stop along I-40 just east of Groom.

Buddy Holly's Footprints
Lubbock

There's a Buddy Holly Center, a Buddy Holly statue, Buddy Holly's Grave, and a Buddy Holly Avenue.

The town is proud of its native son, the rock 'n' roll pioneer of "Peggy Sue" fame who died in a plane crash on February 3, 1959, near Clear Lake, Iowa. The Buddy Holly Center (buddyhollycenter.org; 1801 Crickets Ave.,

Buddy Holly, Lubbock's favorite son PARIS PERMENTER AND JOHN BIGLEY

806-775-3560) is a museum dedicated to the man who brought us "That'll Be the Day" during his short (eighteen-month) but revolutionary career. Located in the renovated Fort Worth & Denver Railroad Depot, the museum had its grand opening in early September 1999.

The centerpiece of the museum? Connie Gibbons, Lubbock's former cultural arts director, figures it would be either Buddy's Fender Stratocaster guitar or Buddy's signature black glasses frames, which have a large case all to themselves. The frames were found at the site of the plane crash.

Also in the museum are one of Buddy's school report cards, his Cub Scout uniform, and his fly rod. "He loved to fish and hunt," Gibbons said. The gift shop has Buddy Holly baseball caps and Buddy Holly T-shirts; it used to have sheet-music boxer shorts.

Was the music accurate on the boxer shorts? "I don't know—we could get a piano and try," Gibbons said.

If that's not enough Buddy Holly stuff for you, you can check out the Buddy Holly Statue, in Buddy Holly Plaza at 1824 Crickets Avenue. The gravesite is at the city cemetery (2011 E. 31st St.), and Lubbock High School (at 2004 19th St.) has a display case full of Holly artifacts in one hall as well as a picture of Holly that's hanging over his homeroom door.

If you visit the high school, please be sure to check in at the principal's office. Buddy Holly probably wouldn't have bothered to do that, but you should.

Stubbs Statue
Lubbock

Like most states, Texas is loaded with statues of generals, tycoons, and politicians. Finally, we get a statue of somebody who did something crucial for humanity—the barbecue man.

The 7-foot bronze of Christopher B. Stubblefield, who everybody called Stubbs, stands at the site of his original barbecue joint at 108 East Broadway. The statue, by Santa Fe sculptor Terry Allen, shows Stubbs as he often was—in overalls and a cowboy hat, holding a plate of ribs.

Stubbs opened his barbecue joint in the late 1960s, and it soon became a favorite hangout for musicians. Joe Ely and Jesse Taylor started a Sunday-night jam session in the place. Artists such as Muddy Waters, Tom T. Hall, and Linda Ronstadt would also show up to play and eat.

In the early 1990s, Stubbs appeared on David Letterman's show and fed barbecue to the studio audience. Stubbs had Letterman eating out of his hand, according to John Scott, who went into business with Stubbs in the 1990s and is one of the founders of Stubb's Barbecue in Austin.

Stubbs in bronze with a plate of his world-famous ribs. VISIT LUBBOCK

"Stubbs just did so well," Scott recalled. "David Letterman said, 'How did you get interested in the art of barbecuing?' Stubbs said, 'My daddy said I was born hungry, so I had to cook.' It just cracked Letterman up."

Stubbs may be gone, but you can still see his face on his statue and on the bottles of his barbecue sauce, which is sold in grocery stores around the world.

Devil's Rope Museum
McLean

This museum devoted to barbed wire (barbwiremuseum.com) is pretty sharp. But it's in the same building as the Route 66 Museum—at 100 Kingsley—for a darned good reason.

"We get 16,000 to 18,000 people going down I-40 each day, and when you see 'Barbwire Museum,' you don't just hit your brakes," said Delbert Trew, supervisor of both museums. "But when you see 'Route 66 Museum,' that's a different deal."

The building where these two museums coexist used to be a brassiere factory called Marie Fashions. So visiting either one should be an uplifting experience. Under the circumstances, I guess it also makes sense that the building houses a pair of museums.

An example of barbed wire art in the Devil's Rope Museum.

The museum exists as a place for barbed wire collectors—there are about 500 of them in the United States, according to Trew—to display their collections. There certainly are plenty of kinds of barbed wire to see in this museum. "There are over 530 patented barbed wires, and we've collected approximately 2,000 variations of those 530 patents," Trew said. In the museum you'll find displays of barbed wire used by planters, barbed wire made for railroads, and barbed wire used in war. Or, in other words, war wire.

In Texas, of course, this would be pronounced "war war."

"Then there are just the plain old machine screw ups, where the machine was worn or missed a lick somewhere, and some people collect those things," Trew said.

There is also barbed wire art in here, including *A Real Sharp Stetson*—a hat made entirely from barbed wire.

"The hat was made by a hippie in Taos, New Mexico, but we didn't get his name," said Trew, who also makes barbed wire art, like the barbed wire jackrabbit and the life-size coyote you'll see in this museum.

You can trade barbs with Trew by calling (806) 779-2225.

The Route 66 Museum
McLean

A chunk of Route 66 still runs through McLean. Up the road from the museum, located at 100 Kingsley (806-779-2225), you'll find an ancient restored Phillips 66 gasoline station. The museum, put together by the Old Route 66 Association of Texas, starts out on a high note with a series of Burma Shave signs by the entrance:

DON'T STICK YOUR

ELBOW OUT SO FAR

IT MIGHT GO HOME

IN ANOTHER CAR

BURMA SHAVE

This could have happened on old Route 66. On the day of my visit, Creed and Wanda Lamb were working as volunteers in the museum. Creed Lamb began running the Lamb Funeral Home in McLean in 1956 and sold the place in 1998. Wanda said Route 66 used to be a real booger. "When we first moved here we had a funeral home, and it was just terrible how many wrecks they had," she said.

If you ask me, the highlight of this museum is the depiction of the 66 Cafe that used to be located on Route 66 in McLean. The re-creation is vintage 1940s or 1950s. You've got a little four-stool counter, dishes set out,

May I take your order?

and a lunch special board that tells you BLTs cost 40 cents. You want to know how dated this joint is? The place even has a cigarette machine.

Among the artifacts you'll see in the museum are some speakers from an old drive-in movie, a life-size doll of a sailor hitchhiking next to a Route 66 sign, and a key from Room 3 at the old Coral Courts Motel. The message by the day or by the hour can be found on this key. So, like the song says, people really did get their kicks on Route 66.

Hanging from the ceiling of The Route 66 Museum is an old road sign that says NINETEEN MILES TO MCLEAN, TEXAS, THE UPLIFT TOWN. The sign, found in a ditch north of town and restored, refers to the fact that McLean was once the home of the aforementioned brassiere factory.

National Cow Calling Championship and Annual Steak Cookoff
Miami

At this annual event, contestants shoot for noise, not for style. Three judges are stationed a half mile to a mile away from the platform where the contestants perform their cow calls. Whoever they can hear the loudest at that distance is the winner.

Don't expect to see cows come arunnin' at the contest, though. Contestants are judged by the volume of their calls, not their effectiveness. The Miami contest is the only such competition in the state and maybe in the country.

The reason this contest goes on here is that the Roberts County community (population: 597) is cattle country, so people are calling their cows anyway. And, as they say, "practice makes perfect."

"You called, I came." PARIS PERMENTER AND JOHN BIGLEY

Post

It is not true that every house in Texas has an oil well in the yard. On the other hand, Post, at the intersection of US 84 and US 380, is the kind of town where people are glad to see the price of gasoline go up. Oil wells are so prevalent that you can sometimes see them operating on the Garza County Courthouse lawn.

Ah, but it was not always this way. In the past, instead of oil, it was bed-sheets and pillowcases. The town of Post was founded in 1907 by eccentric wealthy man C. W. Post, the creator of Post Cereals. Post started the town with the utopian idea of building a model self-contained community.

Post began operations out here when it was buffalo and Indian country. He started by buying about 333 square miles of prairie land. Then he had small farmhouses built and sold them to settlers who wanted to grow cotton.

Post spent $650,000 to build the enormous 444,000-square-foot Postex Cotton Mills, a bedsheet and pillowcase manufacturing plant that had its own cotton gin, boiler operation, and weaving room. The plant was completed in 1911. The farmers living in the little farmhouses would grow the cotton and provide it to Postex. The plant employees would make the sheets.

"It was the first facility that grew the cotton, brought it in to be processed, and made the product all under one facility," said Charles Barker, former

Dan Blocker Bust
O'Donnell

The bronze bust of the big guy who played Hoss Cartwright on the TV western *Bonanza* can be found on a pedestal right across the street from the museum with the Dan Blocker room.

"Nearly everything is right across the street in O'Donnell," said Gustene Bairrington, who was the city secretary.

Dan Blocker grew up in O'Donnell (population: about 1,000). His parents ran the Blocker Grocery. That explains the bronze bust, done by noted sculptor Glenna Goodacre, who also did the Vietnam Women's Memorial.

manager of the town's Old Mill Trade Days. "And marketed the finished product." The plant, later taken over by Burlington Industries, operated until 1983.

J. B. Shewmake, of the town of Tarzan, said his dad worked at the sheet factory in the 1920s and that a tongue twister on this order was posted on one of the plant walls:

I slit a sheet, a sheet I slit,

Upon a slitted sheet I sit.

I'm not a sheet slitter, or a sheet slitter's son,

But I'll slit the sheets 'til the sheet slitter comes.

Say that out loud without screwing up, and you could get yourself a radio job.

Post's stamp can be found all over the town. The beautiful redbrick streets are Post's work. Post's statue is in front of the courthouse. The local paper is called (what else?) the *Post Dispatch*.

Incidentally, Post Trade Day Downtown, takes place along Main Street on the first Saturday of each month. So, if you're lucky, you might be able to buy one of the old bedsheets made by the plant. But I couldn't find that tongue twister.

The O'Donnell Heritage Museum has a pair of Blocker's boxing gloves, a *Bonanza* lunch box, a photo of Blocker's fourth-grade class, and other Hoss Cartwright memorabilia.

They even have a pair of Blocker's Boy Scout pants that he wore at age eleven or twelve. Now in regards to Blocker's Scout pants—they're big for an eleven- or twelve-year-old. Actually, they're big for a forty-year-old. Come to think of it, Blocker's Scout britches may be big enough to house a Cub Scout troop.

So how large are they? "Lord, I don't know. They're big," Bairrington said. "They look to be at least a 46, 48 maybe, but I couldn't tell you for sure."

Musical Welding Job
Pampa

Welder Russell "Rusty" Neef's 150-foot-long steel score of the chorus to Woody Guthrie's "This Land Is Your Land" is so accurate that a musician could read it like a piece of sheet music. And without as much eye strain. The treble clefs are 12 feet high.

"It is musically correct," said Neef, who spent about 400 hours in 1993 creating the work, which can be found on Hobart Street, or TX 70, which runs through the town of Pampa. "You could play it or sing it or whatever, if you knew what you were looking at."

Neef admits he wouldn't know what he was looking at. "I know nothing whatsoever about music," said Neef, a welder since 1946. "That puts me in a very awkward place." So he had Wanetta Hill, a music teacher in the Pampa school system, arrange the score for him in the key of G and 4/4 time.

The reason a Guthrie song was picked for the project? Neef said the folksinger lived in Pampa in the late 1930s and early 1940s. Neef didn't know him well. "But I remember seeing him on the streets," he said. "And he spent some time here. In fact, they like to brag this is where he started writing his music. I don't think that's correct, but it makes a good story."

Neef is proud of his project, which he said should last for eighty to one hundred years because nothing but the best materials were used. "This paint that was put on here was $125 a gallon," said Neef, who spent a little over $18,000 of his own money to build the Guthrie chorus, which he presented to the city. "There wasn't anything on there that was cheap."

Neef said he made the work to leave something behind to honor his father, George Herman Neef, who started the family's welding shop here in 1936. And it's certainly colorful.

"I thought it was so attractive that I lighted it with red, white, and blue lights," Neef said. "It is a patriotic song, so the first section is red, the second one is white, and the third one is blue."

Beard-Growing Contest
Shamrock

The man you have to watch out for in town during the annual beard-growing contest is the Chief Fuzzer. If you don't have a beard on your face, he can have you thrown in the Barefaced Jail.

"Now the whole key is you have to grow the beard," said David Rushing, chairman of the St. Patrick's Committee and city manager of this town of about 2,300 on Route 66. "It's five dollars for the permit. We have the jail on a flatbed. It's a regular old steel jail cell. Some of the welders here in town built it several years ago. If you don't buy the permit, you end up in the jail until you buy it, or you've been in there long enough to grow the Donegal."

Contestants begin growing their Donegal beards—an Irish beard trimmed along the chin line—after they shave clean on January 1 (shamrock texas.net/spd/25-donegal-contest). Then they let their beards grow out for the contest, held the Saturday closest to St. Patrick's Day. Right before the contest, they trim their beards into the Donegal shape. Several of the same faces compete again and again.

Richard Smith, who owns the Route 66 Inn here, said he enters only every ten years to give everybody else a fighting chance. He's won several times. "I think just about every time except the time they imported one from down around Austin somewhere, and he beat me out," Smith added.

Smith is speaking of Scotty McAfee of Austin, who entered the contest one year for the filming of a documentary about the contest, called *Growin' a Beard*. "I've always, you know, had no problem growing hair," McAfee said. In the documentary he is shown trimming his beard as he says, "This is like trying to cut down the Muir Woods with a Weedeater."

The beard-growing contest is to celebrate Shamrock's Irish heritage. A piece of the Blarney Stone from Ireland can be found in town in Elmore Park.

South Texas

South Texas has a deeply intertwined heritage and culture with its south-of-the-border neighbor, Mexico. The interwoven roots of history are evident when you visit the Spanish missions and small villages of South Texas and the Rio Grande Valley. The Institute of Texan Cultures in San Antonio is an excellent place to learn about the different peoples and cultures that influenced this area throughout history.

The largest city in South Texas, San Antonio is the top tourist destination in the state and offers anything and everything to see and do and eat. Of course, the historic Alamo is the most famous of all missions. La Villita, one of San Antonio's original neighborhoods, is now a vibrant showplace of shops, art galleries, and eateries. El Mercado, or Market Square, is the closest thing to shopping in Mexico with its colorful piñatas and Mexican wares.

San Antonio is also an active playground for families with Six Flags Fiesta Texas and SeaWorld San Antonio. The famous, beautifully landscaped River Walk is lined with restaurants offering outstanding Mexican food (duh), steaks, and upscale cuisine, not to mention some of the finest people-watching anywhere.

Kingsville is home to Texas's legendary King Ranch, where a young, adventurous steamboat captain named Richard King established roots in the mid-nineteenth century.

Farther south, the unique ecosystem of the semitropical area known as the Rio Grande Valley attracts nearly 500 species of birds, some not found any place else in the country. Birders and nature lovers flock to the World Birding Center and other nature preserves to try their luck at spotting a green-breasted mango or greater pewee.

The population expands greatly in the winter as thousands of folks from the North escape their frosty homes in RVs and converge on the valley to enjoy its balmy climate.

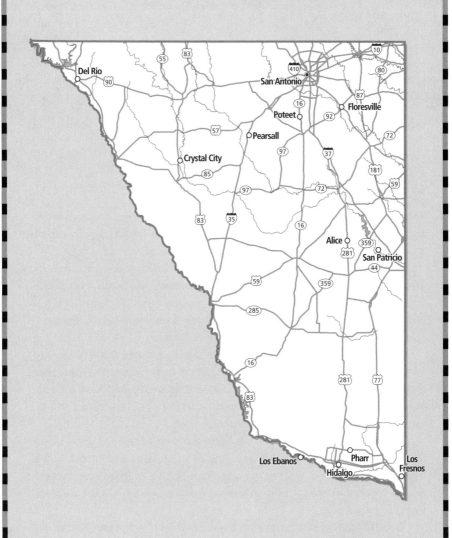

Del Rio
90
55
83
San Antonio
410
10
80
87
Floresville
16
Poteet
92
72
57
Pearsall
97
37
181
Crystal City
85
97
72
59
83
35
16
Alice
359
281
San Patricio
44
59
359
285
16
281
77
83
Los Ebanos
Pharr
Hidalgo
Los Fresnos

0   100 Mi.

0   100 Km.

South Texas

Hope It Doesn't Fall

The 1976 *Guinness World Records* listed the 156-foot water tower as the tallest concrete water tower in the world. Built by the Heldenfels brothers in 1926–27, it still stands near City Hall in downtown Alice. What more can you say about a concrete water tower?

Popeye Statue
Crystal City

The town of Crystal City is forty-eight miles northeast of the Mexican border and a long way from the ocean. So why is a cartoon sailor standing on top of a can of spinach in front of city hall on E. Zavala Street?

Simple. The sailor who gains strength from eating this particular vegetable is shilling for the spinach industry in this town, which bills itself as the Spinach Capital of the World.

"We have a proclamation signed by then President Ronald Reagan," said Christina Flores, the city's former finance director.

It's hard to imagine two towns fighting over spinach, but Crystal City isn't the only place to claim the spinach capital title. "Alma, Arkansas, says they're the Spinach Capital of the World," Flores said. "They have a large-size [statue] of a Popeye. It's similar to the real Popeye in the cartoon strip, but it doesn't quite do the job the way ours does."

Crystal City's Popeye statue has been standing since 1937. Flores said the Crystal City area isn't growing nearly as much spinach as it did in the 1930s and 1940s. Still, the city has a Spinach Festival on the second weekend in November with a spinach cook-off and a Spinach Queen pageant (spinachfestival.org).

Popeye ate his spinach because it was good for him. But he's also smoking a pipe. Seems at cross-purposes, doesn't it?

A fitting mascot for the Spinach Capital of the World.

The Brinkley Mansion

You might want to call this place in Del Rio a quack house. That's because the man who built it, Dr. John R. Brinkley, was perhaps the most colorful and successful quack in the history of the United States.

Brinkley invented the so-called goat gland operation. During his bizarre and checkered career, it was estimated he performed the surgery on more than 16,000 men. For $750, Dr. Brinkley would take the testicle from a Toggenberg goat, sliver it up, then insert a sliver into his patient, which would allegedly cure prostate problems and enhance the patient's sexual performance.

He started the goat gland surgeries in the late 1920s, about the time he moved to the small border town of Del Rio. By the late 1930s, Brinkley had advanced that technique to an injection of fluid. He also sold a line of patent medicines—Nos. 1 through 45, each designed to cure a different ailment.

Brinkley moved to Del Rio so he could build himself a radio station with an extremely powerful signal out of Mexico. The office of XERA (the station's call letters) was in Del Rio, but the transmitter was across the Rio Grande in Via Acuna, where it couldn't be regulated by the U.S. government. In the 1930s, Brinkley would go on the air, talk about religion and

Another Peanut Heard From
Floresville

Nearby Pearsall may have what it claims to be the World's Largest Peanut, but Floresville also has a large peanut statue—on the Wilson County Courthouse lawn, with its own spotlight. About five feet tall, the peanut presents an interesting counterpoint to Lady Justice on top of the courthouse, holding her scales and wearing a blindfold.

The peanut has no such trappings. It is brown and has no face.

politics, sell pieces of the cross of Jesus Christ, and push his medicine. He also was depositing $3,000 a day in the bank just from the sale of his $1 little red paperback book, *Dr. Brinkley's Doctor Book*.

On the air, Brinkley would invite his listeners to come see the show of an evening at the Brinkley House on Qualia Drive, with the two "Dancing Waters" fountains in the front. People would gather in the five-acre park across the street. The water colored with lights would shoot forty feet into the air, go into a mist pattern, and perform other tricks to the sound of Brinkley's 1,063-pipe organ. For the amusement of onlookers, Brinkley's exotic animals—penguins, rare giant Galapagos tortoises, and flamingos—would be released from their pens to roam the grounds.

At one point, to gain accreditation, Brinkley visited Benito Mussolini, the Italian dictator, who got him an honorary degree from a medical school in Rome.

By the late 1930s, people began suing Brinkley, who tried to dodge the bullet by dividing up the estate among his family members, including his wife, Minnie Telitha Brinkley, and son, John "Johnny Boy" Richard Brinkley III. Brinkley died in 1943. By the early 1970s, attorneys suing the family had chewed up all of the money. So Johnny Boy killed himself.

Incidentally, the mansion, at 512 Qualia Dr., is owned by a private family and isn't open to the public. But you can drive by and look.

Designed by local builder Richard Ullmann, the peanut harkens back to a day when many peanuts were grown around these parts. Since 1944, the town has had a weeklong Peanut Festival (floresvillepeanutfestival.org; 830-534-8983) the second week of October, at which a King and Queen Peanut are selected. The queen gets the exotic name of Queen Tunaep.

"The first time I saw that I thought, *What is that poor girl's name?*" said Gwen Fluitt, former executive director of the Floresville Chamber of Commerce. "When I realized it was 'peanut' spelled backward, I said, 'okay,' because I didn't think any parent could be that cruel."

In Floresville they're nuts over peanuts. JIMMY EMERSON, DVM/FLICKR.COM

The king doesn't get off any easier. "The king is 'goober' spelled backward," Fluitt added. "Reboog or whatever. And when they appear at special functions, the king is always wearing a cowboy hat covered in unshelled peanuts, which is kind of peculiar looking."

World's Largest Killer Bee
Hidalgo

The small town of Hidalgo on the Mexican border was the first in Texas to be visited by the deadly bees as they migrated north. So to take the sting out of the situation, the city erected a large (9 1/2 feet by 10 feet by 21 feet) statue to these pests. It's big. It's yellow. It sits in front of City Hall.

And the statue cost the city $16,000 to $17,000. That's a lot of honey.

The killer bees reached Hidalgo on October 15, 1990, according to the sign on the World's Largest Killer Bee.

The killer bees reached Hidalgo on their march north in 1990.

"There was some concern on what kind of negative effect it was going to have on the Rio Grande Valley," said Joe Vera III, former city manager. "I like to say we made lemonade out of lemons. We get thousands who come by every year to have their pictures taken with the bee. It turned a negative into a positive."

Hidalgo's famous giant bee has been in national magazines and newspapers, as well as the *Guinness World Records*. Yes, lemonade indeed.

Hand-Pulled Ferry
Los Ebanos

Want to cross the Rio Grande River into Mexico in an unusual and old-fashioned way?

Well, then, come to this small border town and ride the Los Ebanos Ferry, the last hand-pulled international ferry in the Western Hemisphere. A rope tethered on both banks runs from one side of the river to the other. A crew of four or five guys pulls the ferry across, hand-over-hand.

You could pitch a rock from one side of the river to the other at this location. The trip takes about four minutes one way, costing $7 roundtrip.

Growth has come to Los Ebanos, two miles south of US 83 on FM 886. The ferry holds more cars than the original that opened for business in 1950. The old ferry could hold two cars, but the current ferry can transport three cars.

Who uses this unique ride? Mostly families visiting each other in Mexico and the United States. "And the winter Texans [people from up North who spend winters in Texas] like to come see it," said a U.S. Customs agent. "I guess it's a novelty to see a ferry like this." Be sure to bring your passport if you want to ride!

Hey, will you lend a hand? TEXAS TOURISM/KENNY BRAUN

Alamo Shuffle

If it wasn't for the Daughters of the Republic of Texas, the Alamo in San Antonio might still be a liquor store instead of the state's busiest tourist attraction.

The Alamo went through quite a few changes after it was sacked by Santa Anna on March 6, 1836.

In 1849, the U.S. Army leased the property from the Catholic Church and turned it into a depot. In 1877, Honore Grenet bought the Long Barracks adjacent to the Alamo chapel, leased the chapel, and turned the Long Barracks into a mercantile. The structure, known as Grenet's Castle, had towers and sold wholesale liquor. "But we don't talk about that very much," said Carl McQueary, former director of the Museum for the Daughters of the Republic of Texas in Austin.

In 1882, Grenet died, and in 1886 the Grenet property was sold to Charles Hugo and Gustave Schmeltzer, who, by the early 1900s, were fixing to retire and were looking for a buyer. In stepped the De Zavala Chapter of the Daughters of the Republic of Texas, which began holding fund-raisers to try to raise the $65,000 it would take to purchase the option on the property. But they couldn't raise the money.

Meanwhile, a hotel syndicate from back east was courting Hugo and Schmeltzer to buy the property. So it was looking like the Alamo would be turned into a hotel—until the charming and beautiful Clara Driscoll, a member of the Daughters of the Republic of Texas, stepped in.

McQueary said Driscoll had one other thing going for her. "She had a potful of money," he explained. She was a cattle heiress.

Driscoll put up the $65,000 to buy the property, and the Daughters opened the Alamo to the public in 1908, after a massive cleanup job. Sixteen wagonloads of rubbish had to be removed to put the place back in shape, McQueary said. One wonders how much of that was empty wine bottles.

Little Graceland
Los Fresnos

The late Simon Vega thought so much of Elvis Presley that he named his house Little Graceland. It says so in red letters over the garage door of Vega's little house. If you said anything nasty about Elvis, Vega was liable to get all shook up. He was all goo-goo about the King.

"Very polite, very gracious. He would take a picture with anybody," said Vega, a retired high school teacher, who served in the Army with Elvis from 1958 to 1960 in Freiburg, Germany.

Vega has collected so much Elvis stuff that he had to build a museum for it above his garage. Lighted display cases show off decorative Elvis plates, an Elvis doll dressed in an Army uniform, sunglasses like the ones Elvis wore when he met President Nixon. Vega even has Elvis's good conduct medal.

"I asked him for it. He said, 'Yeah, go ahead. I'll get another one,'" Vega said.

There are also pictures of Vega and Elvis together displayed in his Elvis museum (located on TX 100, 956-233-5482). There's no admission fee to the museum, but donations are accepted.

Every year Vega added a Graceland-style "tribute" to Elvis to his house. The white gate with the green musical notes out front is a must-see. Then there's the stone wall like the one at Graceland that people can come by and sign.

Vega wasn't shy about this. An official state sign on the highway in front of his house identifies the place as Little Graceland. A highway sign on the front lawn reads "Tupelo 85." The arrow on the sign points toward a dog-house-size replica of Elvis's birthplace in Tupelo, Mississippi, that Vega built in his side yard.

The names of Elvis's songs are set in concrete slabs next to Vega's house. Shoot, Vega even wrote a tribute song to Elvis and had it recorded on a 45-rpm record:

"Oh hail to Elvis Presley
You were called the greatest king.
You were called early to heaven,
But your music we will sing."

Every January Vega would throw an Elvis festival for Elvis fans at his house to honor Elvis' birthday. Thousands of people would show up, including a bunch of Elvis impersonators who carried on in an Elvis kind of way.

Vega said, "They come from all over the state. They do their show. They sing. We have a big stage now and a big tent."

World's Largest Peanut

Ironically, the World's Largest Peanut, which really isn't all that large, sits in front of Randall Preston Produce, a potato business on Oak Street in Pearsall.

"Several people come through just to see the peanut," said Juanita Burell, with the Pearsall Chamber of Commerce. "They'll come to the chamber and ask where it's at and if it's accessible."

The town may have the World's Biggest Peanut, but it has a Potato Festival instead of a Peanut Festival. The Peanut Festival is in Floresville.

"We do grow quite a bit of potatoes here," Juanita said. "In fact, Frito-Lay buys all the potatoes. It's sixteen hours from the field into a bag of chips. It doesn't take 'em long, that's for sure. But we still do produce quite a bit of peanuts."

The reason the peanut is here, of course, is that Pearsall is in a peanut-growing area. PEARSALL, TEXAS—WORLD'S LARGEST PEANUT—55,000,000 LBS. MARKETED ANNUALLY, it says on the peanut's concrete base.

Unfortunately, the January 2018 Elvis Festival was cancelled in light of Simon Vega's passing in May 2017, followed by the passing of his wife Teresa in November. While you can certainly still drive by the house, the museum has been closed until further notice. Updates can be sought out via the phone number listed above.

Smitty's Jukebox Museum
Pharr

Enter another age and wallow in nostalgia when you go into this small, non-descript building (one of the oldest in Pharr) along the railroad tracks. Owner Leo Schmidt Jr. (Smitty Jr.) will take you on a tour down memory lane. His father began Smitty's Music and Amusement Company in 1947, long before anyone had heard of iPods and iTunes. The family business sold, leased, and serviced jukeboxes and other coin-operated machines. Over the years, the elder Smitty found himself keeping many of them.

The exceptional collection spans the ages of music machines, from a wind-up Edison Victrola to modern touch-tone digital players that can download 800,000 selections.

Smitty Jr. welcomes visitors and always acts like he was just waiting for you to come in. He loves to talk about his treasures, all lovingly restored by him and/or his dad. "This is the oldest; it's a 1926 Electra-muse," he said proudly. "You could choose from eight records for a nickel."

Hanging out in the place and listening to Smitty is an extraordinary history lesson. "This Wurlitzer was made in 1942. They stopped production when the war came along."

There was a time when you could go into just about any dance hall, diner, restaurant, or bar and buy music for a nickel from machines sporting names like Wurlitzer, Rock-Ola, and Seeburg. During the golden age of

Smitty's jukeboxes have been lovingly restored.

jukeboxes, the music machines themselves were works of art displaying brilliant colors, flashing and shimmering bulbs, fluorescent lights that changed colors, and sparkling bubble tubes.

"Do you want to see my 45-rpm record collection?" Smitty Jr. asked. Silly question. He opened the door to another room—oh, my! "I have more than 100,000, about half in English and half in Spanish." Amazingly, he knows where each one is.

When his dad died in 2000, Smitty Jr. took over. He doesn't sell many jukeboxes these days, but he does restore and repair them in his open workshop (116 W. State St.; 956-787-0131).

As I started to leave, a song wandered through my mind—Mark Chesnutt singing "Bubba Shot the Jukebox."

World's Largest Strawberry
Poteet

In Texas, if we don't have the largest plant growing naturally, we just build one and call it the world's largest. We will stop at nothing to be biggest, doggone it, in the Lone Star State.

The World's Largest Strawberry weighs 1,600 pounds, stands 7 feet, 3 inches tall, is mostly red, and sits right in front of the Poteet Volunteer Fire Department, where it doesn't clash with the fire trucks.

According to Nita Harvey, former coordinator of the annual Strawberry Festival (strawberryfestival.com; 830-742-8144) here in the Strawberry Capital of Texas, the World's Largest Strawberry is made out of "some kind of plaster."

The World's Largest Strawberry is among several other world's largest-growing item statues to be found around Texas.

The statue is part of a set of huge strawberries here—the other one being the town's 130-foot-tall water tower, which is, you got it, shaped like a strawberry. "It's billed as the World's Tallest Strawberry," Harvey said.

While in Seguin, you'll have a hard time missing what was once billed as the World's Largest Pecan, because it weighs one thousand pounds, is made out of concrete, and sits in the Guadalupe County Courthouse square.

Poteet strawberries are known for their sweetness.

PARIS PERMENTER AND JOHN BIGLEY

The chupacabra legend may have begun in Mexico and south Texas but its influence now spreads across the state, as in this bar in Austin.

Chupacabra
Rio Grande Valley

This devil-like creature comes to your ranch at night and sucks the blood out of your goats.

Chupacabra means "goat sucker" in Spanish. The legend came to the Rio Grande Valley and Mexico via Puerto Rico, said Dr. Mark Glazer, retired anthropology professor at the University of Texas–Pan American (now known as The University of Texas Rio Grande Valley) in Edinburg.

Any evidence of dead goats sucked dry? "Not really," said Glazer, who described chupacabra as "a pseudo-zoological entity, much like the Loch Ness monster or Bigfoot."

As he explained it, "All of these legends and rumors and urban legends simply go around as a rumor mechanism." The reason the monster is said to suck goats, Glazer said, is that a lot of goat meat is consumed in the valley.

Such scary stories are common to the region. "This area already had a big bird," Glazer said of a chupacabra predecessor. "It's supposed to be a huge prehistoric bird flying around."

The looks of chupacabra changed as the story migrated. "In Puerto Rico it looks like a space alien, with big eyes and a triangular face," Glazer said. "In Puerto Rico, in its earlier forms, it's basically said to be a pet left over by aliens. So to survive on Earth, it sucks goats' blood."

As chupacabra tales moved into the Rio Grande Valley, the creature began to look like a demon about three feet tall. And its diet became more varied. "People began to see them at ranches attacking not only goats but chickens as well," Glazer said.

The Alamo City
San Antonio

It's not hard to tell from looking in the business listings of the San Antonio phone book that San Antonio might be known as the Alamo City. Starting with the actual Alamo, located in downtown San Antonio, you've got about four pages of names that start with Alamo. Just about any kind of business you can imagine in this city uses Alamo as part of its name.

Looking for lunch? Head to the Alamo Café. Having trouble sleeping? Call the Alamo Sleep Center & Respiratory Equipment. Trying to stop an

Reminders of San Antonio's biggest attraction are all over town.
PARIS PERMENTER AND JOHN BIGLEY

itch? Then call the Alamo Area Dermatology Associates. Getting run out of town? Call Alamo Mayflower.

Davy Crockett might have had a hard time figuring out what some of these businesses are for. Imagine Crockett walking into the Alamo Acupuncture & Chinese Herbal Clinic.

Then you've got the Alamo Area Speech Language & Swallowing Services, Alamo Strip-A-Dancer, Alamo Bail Bonds, Alamo Backhoe Service, Alamo Bathtub Refinishing, Alamo Bone & Joint Clinic, Alamo Paper Tube Co., Alamo City Bed & Breakfast Hotline, Alamo City Tall Club, Alamo Dog Obedience Club, Alamo City Mortuary Service, Alamo Shaver & Appliance, Alamo Mold Inspection, and Alamo City Paranormal, to name a few.

The Wooden Nickel Historical Museum
San Antonio

How many times a day did the late museum owner Herb Hornung hear the old joke about not taking any wooden nickels?

"Sometimes between twenty and thirty times a day," said Herb, who was a retired Air Force technician and a wooden nickel expert who collected wooden nickels since he was a kid. "And the other one is: Do we have any round tuits?"

The answer is, yes, they do have a "round tuit" available. The Old Time Wooden Nickel Company, (wooden-nickel.com; 210-822-0552) makes and sells about 5 million wooden nickels a year, including the round tuits, wooden nickels with "TUIT" printed on one side and the message "DO IT WHEN YOU GET AROUND TO IT!" on the other.

If you wanted to know about wooden nickels, Herb was your guy. He could tell you all about how the "Don't take any wooden nickels" expression got started. It popped up in the 1930s when fair customers in Chicago redeemed wooden nickels for fair fare. On the last day of the fair when the nickels were about to expire, people would remind one another to "not take any wooden nickels," since they were about to turn worthless. Or so they thought. Actually, these tokens would become collectors' items.

"'Course, the people who couldn't cash them in were the real winners, 'cause these are worth between $5 and $10 now," Herb said.

Although Herb Hornung passed away in 2008, his interest in wooden nickels lives on in his factory and museum. The museum has about 1.5 million wooden nickels on hand, with about 10,000 of them on display, including wooden nickels ordered as business cards by Henny Youngman, Jack Paar, and Red Skelton. There are wooden nickels good for ONE FREE SALAD at Pizza Hut. And political wooden nickels, like the one touting Jimmy Carter for president.

The factory makes wooden nickels for all kinds of customers: bands named Wooden Nickel, bars and restaurants named Wooden Nickel, motorcycle clubs, golf courses, Moose Clubs, casinos, even orthodontists.

Then there's the World's Largest Wooden Nickel that Herb built out of lumber. It sits outside near the front door. You shouldn't take this one, either, because it'll give you a hernia. It's more than 13 feet in diameter and weighs 2,500 pounds.

The World's Largest Wooden Nickel weighs over a ton.
PARIS PERMENTER AND JOHN BIGLEY

The Wooden Nickel Historical Museum is at 345 Old Austin Road, open 9a.m. to 5 p.m. Monday through Thursday. Look for the gigantic wooden nickel marking the spot.

Barney Smith's Toilet Seat Art Museum
San Antonio

This museum consists mostly of toilet seat lids decorated by Barney Smith, a retired master plumber who is now in his nineties.

At last count, Smith had nearly 1,000 toilet seats and lids in his garage at 239 Abiso Ave. in the San Antonio suburb of Alamo Heights (facebook.com/SATXTSAM; 210-824-7791). Each item has a different theme. Some themes are more serious than others.

Barney Smith turns toilet seats into works of art. JULIEGOMOLL/FLICKR.COM

One decorated toilet seat in the museum, Smith said, is a number called The Pooch Parade, honoring a dog walk held in Alamo Heights.

"They start at the swimming pool and they walk for several blocks," Smith said.

Deceased hornets are glued to one toilet seat and lid combination. Please open slowly, Do NOT DISTURB, reads the message on the lid. Lift the lid and you see the bugs underneath. "These are yellow jackets," Smith said. "One of them stung me on my head, and I just said, 'I'll put you on my toilet seat.'" Now that's what I call a payback.

Another lid has a photo of Miss America on it. (Miss America probably didn't figure she'd end up being so honored, right?) Another toilet seat lid is covered with dog tags (from dogs, not soldiers), and still another is decorated with somebody's collection of swizzle sticks.

Smith selected toilet seats as his motif because he has connections in the plumbing supply business who give him damaged toilet seats they can't sell. He said the neighbors don't complain because the garage museum hasn't attracted a lot of tour buses.

Ironically, the museum has no bathroom. "I got plenty of toilet seats, but no toilet," Smith admitted.

Buckhorn Saloon & Museum
San Antonio

Who says Texans brag too much? If it wasn't for Texans running their mouths, this collection of over 1,500 horns and animal mounts wouldn't exist.

The "world's greatest collection of horns and antlers" started in 1881, when patrons of the Buckhorn Saloon, who were at another downtown location in San Antonio at the time, started boasting about the critters they had bagged while hunting. Albert Friedrich, the saloon's founder, told his customers, in so many words, "Dandy. Let's see what you've got."

"They'd brag about how big their horns were, and he'd say, 'Bring 'em in,'" said Kristi Engelman, the museum's former sales manager.

Engelman said Friedrich would give his patrons free beer and whiskey in exchange for allowing him to display their hunting trophies in his tavern. Friedrich used the collection to keep the saloon afloat during Prohibition. He started selling non-alcoholic drinks and people began coming to see the collection.

San Antonio's Buckhorn Saloon & Museum is famous for its collection of antlers and other artifacts. SAN ANTONIO CONVENTION AND VISITORS BUREAU

During the Depression, Friedrich's wife Emile accepted jars of rattle-snake rattles as drink payments and she began crafting rattle artwork, which is still on display.

The museum is at 318 East Houston St. (buckhornmuseum.com; 210-247-4000).

Pig Stand No. 29
San Antonio

If it wasn't for the Pig Stand chain, Americans might never have figured out how to eat in their cars.

The chain claims to be the world's first drive-in. A bunch of Pig Stands—along with this one, back then at a nearby location—popped up the 1920s. At one point there were Pig Stands coast to coast. Now just the Pig Stand in San Antonio remains.

If you don't start oinking after you visit this place at 1508 Broadway (san antoniospigstand.com; 210-222-9923), you're not paying attention. Ceramic and plaster pigs decorate the interior. One pig is in cowboy clothes and another in overalls. A red and green neon pig—a 6-foot-long, 4-foot-tall

Pig Stand No. 29 is the last of its kind. PARIS PERMENTER AND JOHN BIGLEY

number made in 1924—hangs from the ceiling. It's one of the oldest neon signs in the nation. I recommend the Pig Sandwich combo: a sliced pork sandwich on a bun with fries and slaw. You might also try the chocolate malt, named the best in San Antonio by the *Current*, a local weekly paper.

The Pig Stand makes a lot of claims about having the first this and the first that. Kathy Racicot, former manager of Pig Stand No. 29, said the Pig Stand introduced curb service, onion rings, Texas toast, fluorescent and neon lighting at restaurants, and chicken-fried steak.

Wait a minute. The Pig Stand invented chicken-fried steak? That's a pretty major claim, lady.

Kathy amended that to say the Pig Stand introduced the chicken-fried steak sandwich. I said that wasn't quite such a tall brag. "Still counts," she said. "And onion rings was a biggy." Yes, it was.

The last Pig Stand is owned by Mary Ann Hill, who began working as a waitress at the Broadway Pig Stand back in 1967 when she was eighteen, and has been an employee at the eatery ever since.

Really Big Fake Cowboy Boots
San Antonio

These boots—billed as the biggest cowboy boots in the world—weren't made for walking. But they weren't made for living in, either. On the other hand, the 40-foot-tall boots installed by Austin artist Bob "Daddy-O" Wade at the North Star Mall at San Pedro Avenue and Loop 410 are so big that a wino once moved into one of them.

Wade, who makes large art out of polyurethane, said a cowboy had kicked a hole in one of the boots, making it possible for someone to move in.

"At one point I got a call claiming that the boots were on fire," Wade recalled. The reason for the smoke? A homeless guy had taken up residence in one of the boots and was doing a little cooking inside. "He was heating up hot dogs with Sterno," said Wade.

The homeless guy was booted out. (I'd like to get the name of the heel who evicted him.) "They should have left him," Wade said. "They messed up. The tourists would have loved him."

Certainly the boots are big enough to serve as a condo. Wade said the boots are thirty feet from toe to heel. "We figured out they will hold 300,000 gallons of beer each," he added.

Going to the mall to see the big boots was named one of "The 10 Dumbest Things to Do in San Antonio" by the *New York Daily News*.

These boots were (definitely not) made for walking.
SAN ANTONIO CONVENTION AND VISITORS BUREAU/AL RENDON

Coincidentally, the mention was made shortly before the San Antonio Spurs booted the New York Knicks square in the butt in the NBA finals.

World Championship Rattlesnake Races
San Patricio

So what's the big tip on how to get a rattlesnake to race?

"Just don't make 'em mad," said the late Larry Belcher, an eighteen-wheeler driver from Alice who won this annual event (wcrattlesnakeraces .com) three times with his rattlesnake, Sleepy. "If you make 'em mad, they're gonna curl up and try to bite you."

Some people, as Belcher did, bring their own snakes and race them. Other race snakes are provided by snake hunters.

The rattlesnakes race in lanes. The course—about 80 feet long—is lined. To get the rattlesnakes going, racers tap the ground next to their snakes with 5-foot-long plastic tubes called "go-gitters." "That vibration of the ground will make them move," said Jim Dulaney, former president of the San Patricio Restoration Society, the event's sponsor.

The races have been going on every year since 1972. They're held to celebrate St. Patrick's Day. As we all know, St. Patrick drove the snakes out of Ireland. Get it?

Sometimes the rattlesnakes move briskly. Sometimes they just sit there and goof off. "We put in a new rule that if it takes over fifteen minutes, the one that's ahead is declared the winner, because the people start getting bored," Dulaney explained.

Each racer is assigned a handler who has a spring-loaded snake-grabbing tool. If the snake strays out of the lane, the handler grabs it by the neck and puts it back on course.

No contestants have been bitten so far, although some of the handlers have been nailed.

It's the other end you should worry about. PARIS PERMENTER AND JOHN BIGLEY

Gulf Coast

Known for its wildlife and natural beauty, the Texas Gulf Coast is a long, narrow strip stretching 367 miles along the Gulf of Mexico from the Louisiana border to South Padre Island. This playground connects picturesque beaches, parks, wildlife preserves, peninsulas, and islands, as well as seaside cities and towns.

A popular tourist destination, Galveston provides all anyone could want in the way of fun in the sun, family entertainment, and shopping in its restored historic district chock-a-block full of antiques stores, art galleries, and eateries. Mother Nature has tried to destroy the historic city of Galveston more than once, but its tenacious character is legendary.

Corpus Christi, the largest city along the Gulf Coast, offers fabulous sport fishing, windsurfing, sailing, birding, and pretty much any outdoor activity. Family attractions include the cutting edge Texas State Aquarium and the USS Lexington, a World War II–era aircraft carrier moored in Corpus Christi Bay.

All along the coast, small cities and towns such as Port Aransas, Rockport, and Port Isabel are noted for excellent deep-sea fishing and water recreation such as kayaking, surfing, swimming, and birding. Aransas National Wildlife Refuge (near Rockport) is the winter nesting ground of the only natural wild flock of whooping cranes, one of the rarest birds in North America.

If you'd like more solitude, head for Padre Island National Seashore, the longest undeveloped stretch of barrier island in the world, with seventy miles of sandy beaches.

Perhaps the best known vacation destination is South Padre Island, a coastal resort offering something for everyone in the family. High-rise hotels and kitschy souvenir shops line the island, but there are also beautiful beaches, riding stables, water parks, and even bungee jumping. Restaurants offer everything from haute cuisine to chicken-fried fill-in-the-blank.

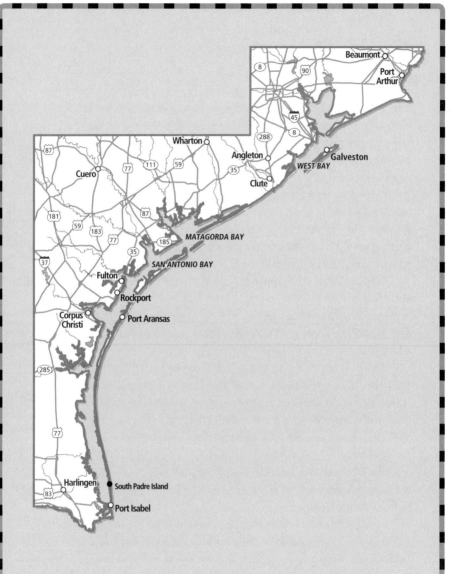

Beaumont

Port
Arthur

Wharton

Angleton

Galveston

Cuero

Clute

WEST BAY

MATAGORDA BAY

SAN ANTONIO BAY

Fulton

Rockport

Port Aransas

Corpus
Christi

Harlingen

South Padre Island

Port Isabel

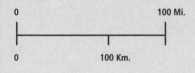

0   100 Mi.

0   100 Km.

Gulf Coast

Stephen F. Austin Statue
Angleton

Built by the same sculptor who constructed the Texas-sized Sam Houston in Huntsville, the Stephen F. Austin statue is hard to miss. The tribute to the Father of Texas stands 60 feet tall on a 12-foot base just off Highway 35 on Highway 288. The nearby visitor's center is open 9 a.m. to 6 p.m. Wednesday through Sunday.

The work is by Houston sculptor David Adickes who is also known for his series of gargantuan presidential heads. According to the *Wall Street Journal*, "David Adickes looms large in the art world—and for no small reason. His gigantic statues of historical figures have become tourist attractions from South Dakota to Virginia to his home state of Texas."

The Texas-sized Father of Texas. PARIS PERMENTER AND JOHN BIGLEY

The Big Bopper
Beaumont

Is there an American over the age of fifty who doesn't remember these lyrics?

"Chantilly lace and a pretty face

And a ponytail hanging on down.

A wiggle in the walk, and a giggle in the talk,

Make the world go round."

Those words were written in a car headed from Beaumont to Houston by the late Jiles Perry Richardson, aka the Big Bopper, according to John Neil, now deceased, who used to have an ad agency in Beaumont called John Neil Advertising.

In the late 1940s, Neil and Richardson worked together at KTRM-AM in Beaumont. Richardson was the night DJ (known as the Night Mare), and Neil was the engineer.

In the 1950s the Big Bopper's "Chantilly Lace" would make it to the top of the charts. That it got there was a fluke.

"He wrote that song on his way to Houston to record 'The Purple People Eater Meets the Witch Doctor,' " said Neil. See, the Big Bopper had to come up with a B-side for the 45-rpm record he was about to record. "The Purple People Eater Meets the Witch Doctor" was the A-side. So he wrote "Chantilly Lace" for the B-side. And that's the one that hit the charts.

Neil recalls the Big Bopper fondly. "He was kind of a laid back fella. He couldn't sing, and he couldn't play the guitar. But he could put on a show," said Neil. "He wore this zoot suit, and when he got off the stage you could almost wring that suit out."

Neil's father Jack founded and ran the radio station. He'd be trying to write his newscast in the station's studio A, while J. P. was attempting to play the guitar and piano.

"And Daddy would say, 'Goddamn it, J. P., put the goddamn guitar down and go out and get yourself a beer or something,'" Neil remembered, "And J. P. would go down to the Quality Cafe and get a beer."

In 1959, the Big Bopper died in a plane crash near Clear Lake, Iowa, with Ritchie Valens and Buddy Holly. The people at the station were devastated when they found out. "Daddy just laid his head down on the desk and started cryin'," Neil said. "And that was the first and only time I ever saw my daddy cry."

At the funeral a photographer working for *Life* magazine brought along a couple of teenage gals to use as props.

The modest grave of Jiles Perry Richardson, aka the Big Bopper ROBERT BROWN

"He had them draped over J. P.'s casket crying, to take a picture of him," Neil said. "He thought it would make a good picture, but he couldn't take the picture 'cause we kept his camera."

There She Blows!
Beaumont

It's not just every place you get to see a gusher—but lucky visitors at Spindle-top Gladys City Boomtown Museum (spindletop.org; Lamar University, 5550 Jimmy Simmons Blvd., 409-880-1750) can see the Lucas Gusher at scheduled times. Sitting just off Highway 69, the gusher blows water hundreds of feet in the air.

The Lucas Gusher blows its top several times a day.
BEAUMONT CONVENTION & VISITORS BUREAU

The Lucas Gusher—named for the Australian-born engineer and financier of Spindletop drilling—came in at 10:30 a.m. on January 10, 1901. The gusher was the best oil well that had ever been seen, estimated to flow 80,000 to 100,000 barrels per day, and signaled the start of the U.S. oil industry.

Today the Lucas Gusher spouts water at the same rate as that original gusher spouted oil over a century ago. Check the Gladys City Facebook page (facebook.com/GladysCity) for the next scheduled display.

World's Largest (Working) Fire Hydrant
Beaumont

I just had to ask: Do folks walk their dogs around the World's Largest Working Fire Hydrant, located outside the Fire Museum of Texas? "Uh, no," said Susan Lanning, the museum's former director. Then what's the matter with them? If I lived in Beaumont and if I didn't have a dog, I'd go get one just because of this artwork.

The Dalmatian-decorated hydrant is a BIG attraction in Beaumont.
BEAUMONT CONVENTION & VISITORS BUREAU

Well, it *was* the world's largest fire hydrant when it was built in 1999, but some folks just can't let a world's record alone. So in 2001, larger ones appeared in Columbia, South Carolina, and Elm Creek, Manitoba.

Walt Disney Company built the 24-foot-tall fiberglass fire hydrant to promote its *101 Dalmatians* movie, which explains the hydrant's black-and-white-spotted paint job. Disney "did this whole media event," Lanning recalled. "They had over one hundred local firefighters dressed up in their turnout gear carrying Dalmatian-spotted umbrellas, and they did a dance routine."

"It shoots water out of the top like a sprinkler system," Lanning said. So today this is the world's largest fire hydrant that actually works.

The hydrant may not attract a lot of beagles and their owners, but it does bring a bunch of people with cameras and may be the most photographed attraction in town. "The fire hydrant—it's like our giant ball of twine," said Timothy Kelly, editor of the *Beaumont Enterprise*, the town's daily newspaper. "I've watched minivans pull up, people jump out and take a picture, then move on. It's pretty funny."

Kelly said it isn't unusual for Disney to put up promotional stuff around these parts. He recalled a fabric Great Wall of China that Disney constructed in nearby China, Texas, to promote the movie *Mulan*.

"It was humongous," said former China City Secretary Jerry Howard. "I forget how long that thing was. It was at least 100 to 200 feet long."

The Fire Museum of Texas (fmotassn.com; 400 Walnut St., 409-880-3927) is not only an exceptional museum exhibiting vintage equipment and memorabilia, but is also the headquarters of the Beaumont Fire Department.

Turkeyfest
Cuero

Often called the "Turkey Capital of the World," it's hard to miss the turkey connection in this South Texas town. Cuero's high school football team is the Gobblers, and the town's biggest event is the annual Turkeyfest (turkeyfest.org).

Although a sighting of what many claim to be the mythical Chupacabra brought national attention to the small southeast Texas town of Cuero in the summer of 2007, poultry is the true passion of DeWitt County denizens. Each second weekend of October folks flock to Cuero for some "fowl" festivities during a three-day salute to the town's farming origins.

No festival would be complete without a few friendly competitions. Weekend grillers turn up the heat in a bid to be the festival's supreme sizzler in the BBQ cook-off, while other inspiring chefs cook up taste bud–tempting ingredients in the chili and jackpot bean cook-offs. For eye-watering entertainment, participants try to polish off as many peppers as possible in the jalapeno eating contest.

Athletically adept attendees will enjoy the volleyball tournament and the 5K Turkey Trot, while others will be content to sit back and enjoy the live music entertainment.

Cuero is talkin' turkey. PARIS PERMENTER AND JOHN BIGLEY

The crowning moment of this fowl-tempered festival, however, is the Great Gobbler Gallop. Residents and visitors gather round to root for the trotting turkey as it races against the clock in an attempt to beat the time set by rival Worthington, Minnesota's prized poultry. An event hatched back in 1912, today's version of the Great Gobbler Gallop has garnered the attention of the media and has been showcased on the Food Network and the *CBS Sunday Morning* show.

The Great Texas Mosquito Festival
Clute

It's held the last Thursday, Friday, and Saturday in July to honor the huge mosquito population here in Clute (mosquitofestival.com; 979-265-8392).

"We still have a tremendous amount of them," said Dana Pomerenke, director of the Clute Parks and Recreation Department, speaking about the bug population in December. "They ate me up last night in my own yard."

Why not head to Clute to visit with Willie Manchew (shown here) for the Great Texas Mosquito Festival? TOM FOWLER LJTX/FLICKR.COM

The festival highlights are a mosquito-calling contest, the crowning of Mister and Miss Skeeter, and a mosquito leg look-alike contest. "You don't do a costume," Pomerenke said of the leg look-alike contest. "It's your legs, so it's usually the most skinny, hairy legs that win." The event is held at Clute Parks and Recreation, home of Willie Manchew, a 25-foot-tall inflatable mosquito.

The Selena Statue
Corpus Christi

Here in Texas we do a great job of honoring our deceased music icons when they die young and tragically. Lubbock has the Buddy Holly statue, Austin has the Stevie Ray Vaughan statue, and Corpus Christi has a bronze statue of hometown gal Selena, the beloved star Tejano singer who was murdered by her fan club president.

Tejano icon Selena is remembered near Corpus Christi's Peoples Street T-Head.
PARIS PERMENTER AND JOHN BIGLEY

Yolanda Saldivar shot Selena in 1995 at the Days Inn on Navigation Boulevard. In Corpus, Selena is regarded by some almost as a religious figure. On the day of her funeral, the city's daily newspaper, the *Corpus Christi Caller-Times*, ran a special section with a photo of her in her casket on the back page. To bring closure, the five-shot, .38 caliber Taurus revolver used to murder Selena was cut into about fifty pieces and dumped into Corpus Christi Bay.

The statue, set up under a gazebo, is a good likeness of Selena. But the face is solemn.

The artist, H. W. Tatum, "did a couple of features," said Dusty Durrill, who built the gazebo site. "We had two heads. One, she was smiling, and one, she was solemn, and the family wanted the solemn head."

Selena's Grave

Selena Quintanilla-Pérez, better known to the world as Selena, was murdered in Corpus Christi on March 31, 1995, at the age of twenty-three. The Tejano, Latin pop, and pop star is remembered at several sites in the city including the Selena Museum (q-productions.com; 5410 Leopard St., 361-289-9013) and a memorial at the entrance to the People's Street T-Head.

Many travelers stop to pay their respects at Selena's grave; she is buried in the Seaside Memorial Park in Corpus Christi at 4357 Ocean Dr. From the entrance to the cemetery, turn left; Selena's grave is recognizable by its stone fence and is often visited by travelers.

PARIS PERMENTER AND JOHN BIGLEY

The grave is topped with a relief of Selena; behind the grave a small bench under a tall oak tree provides a quiet place for family members to reflect on the star's life.

The smiling head is on display at the Corpus Christi Museum of Science and History at 1900 North Chaparral.

Just about any time you go by the statue, located on the sea wall on North Shoreline Boulevard at Peoples Street, you'll see people visiting it. At about 7:00 a.m. on a chilly Sunday morning, Troy Price from Alabama had come by to take a picture of the Selena statue for his fourteen-year-old son back home. The kid is a big fan.

"You never know how big she could have been," Price said. "Not many performers are known by their first name only, and she was already there. You got Madonna. And Elvis. Everybody knows who Elvis is."

Fulton Mansion
Fulton

"The kids coming in here, they're all screaming 'cause it looks like the Munsters," said Charlie Cook, retired tour guide for this spooky-looking Second Empire French home built in the 1870s by longhorn cattle magnate George Ware Fulton.

People in town think this place is haunted. The story I heard from the locals is that one of Fulton's daughters died young, so she prowls the mansion at night.

"They say she stands up there in the window," said Melanie Vaughan, a former employee in the nearby Boiling Pot seafood restaurant. Melanie said she saw the ghost in the bathroom when she was a kid. "I swear I saw the ghost in the bathroom, but I believe in that kind of stuff," Melanie said.

Cook pointed out that neither of Fulton's two daughters died young. Annie and Hattie both lived to a ripe old age, he said. There is no ghost, but don't try to tell that to the locals.

Designated a State Historic Site, Fulton Mansion is open to the public for tours.
PARIS PERMENTER AND JOHN BIGLEY

"We've got people in this community, they still think this house is haunted," said Buck Spurlock, formerly a park ranger here. Now the Texas Historical Commission operates the renovated mansion (visitfultonmansion .com; 317 Fulton Beach Rd., 361-729-0386) as a tourist attraction. "I've been in here at night, and it does squeak a little bit."

Maybe Lillian "Big Mamma" Davidson started the ghost rumors. The Davidson family of San Antonio bought the Fulton Mansion after George Fulton died in 1893. Big Mamma lived in the place from 1907 to 1943, Charlie said.

"The Davidson kids would invite their friends in this house, and Big Mamma would dress up as a ghost and scare them to death," Charlie said. "She would go to the high school and tell ghost stories about the place."

Then there is the fact that the place sat around empty, collecting dust and spider webs for years, until the state began restoring it in 1976.

It probably doesn't help, either, that the marker out front of the house says that George Fulton died on October 31, 1893—Halloween. That's a mistake, Charlie said. George Fulton really died October 30.

Maybe the state made the mistake on purpose to attract tourists. Either way, if you're going to tour the place, bring your own ghost.

The Fulton Mansion was damaged by the devastating strength of Hurricane Harvey in the summer of 2017. Though it sustained damage, it remained standing, marking its survival though eight hurricanes. The museum was closed for repairs until March 2018, when it was reopened for "hard hat tours," allowing guests to walk through rooms typically blocked off in the museum's normal operation, while construction continues. The Education and History Center remains open as usual during construction.

Giant Crab and Shrimp
Galveston

The late Rick Gaido, who was director of operations for Gaido's, perhaps the best seafood place in the state (3900 Seawall Blvd.; 409-761-5500), once pointed out that "people rarely remember our name, but they do remember it's the restaurant with the crab on the roof."

So to attract customers to Casey's (recently renamed Nick's Kitchen & Beach Bar), the restaurant next door, at 3800 Seawall Blvd., which is also owned by Gaido's, they put up a large pink shrimp. The crab has been up for years, while the shrimp is a fairly recent addition.

Actually, the shrimp isn't on the roof. It's on a pole. It's big and pink and has bulging eyes. "A lot of people think it's a crawfish," Rick said. Yeah, well, a lot of people aren't from Louisiana.

Giant shrimp: oxymoron or just good advertising?

The crab is a blue-claw crab with a sign on it that says CAUGHT IN GALVESTON BAY. As big as it is, if it had been caught in Galveston Bay, scientists would have to check the bay for nuclear radiation.

"We'll say it's real, and you'd be surprised how many people believe it," Rick said.

You can visit the restaurant websites at gaidos.com or nicksgalveston.com.

"Wrong Way" Corrigan

Perhaps no man in America brings the word "whoops" to mind as strongly as the late Douglas Corrigan, a Galveston native son. Corrigan was supposed to be headed in his single-engine airplane from New York to Long Beach, California, on July 17, 1938, but ended up landing in Dublin, Ireland, twenty-nine hours after taking off.

Corrigan was born in Galveston on January 22, 1907, according to Shelly Henley Kelly, former assistant archivist with the Rosenberg Library in Galveston. In May 1908, Corrigan won a cute baby contest in Galveston. At age fifteen, he changed his name from Clyde Groce Corrigan to Douglas Corrigan, after actor Douglas Fairbanks.

But the name change was all for naught, because after he got going in his plane all bassackwards, he would be called Wrong Way Corrigan for the rest of his life.

Corrigan had wanted to fly across the Atlantic like Charles Lindbergh did. (In fact, Corrigan had worked as an aircraft mechanic for Lindbergh.) But his plane was such a heap of junk, Kelly said, that flight officials wouldn't give him a flight plan to cross the big pond. So he filed a flight plan that had him headed to California.

"It's a crate, is how they described it," Kelly said of Corrigan's 1929 Curtiss-Robin airplane. "This guy had his door held shut with baling wire. And he didn't have many instruments. He had two compasses, and that was it."

After ending up in Ireland, Corrigan blamed his equipment. "His excuse was one of the compasses froze up and broke, and the other one was broken 180 degrees," Kelly said. Corrigan was sent back to the United States by boat.

The goof didn't stop Galveston from bringing Corrigan back to town on August 26, 1938, for a ticker-tape parade. The Galveston airport was renamed for him, though Kelly said it might have been just for the day. There was even a song about Corrigan written and published by Eloise Drake of Galveston. The song was called, "If Your Compass Is Turned Around."

Iwo Jima Model
Harlingen

Just steps away from the airport lies one of Harlingen's most unique attractions: the Iwo Jima Monument and Memorial Museum. Located across the street from the Iwo Jima Memorial Museum (320 Iwo Jima Blvd.; 956-421-9234), this statue was the working model for the bronze statue in Arlington National Cemetery.

32-foot-high figures make up the famous statue. PARIS PERMENTER AND JOHN BIGLEY

The model took nearly ten years for sculptor Dr. Felix W. de Weldon to complete; it was then dismantled and shipped to Brooklyn to be cast in bronze. The model was then taken to Dr. de Weldon's summer home in Rhode Island where it remained until 1982 when it was erected on the parade grounds of Harlingen's Marine Military Academy.

Castles in the Sand
Port Aransas

Visit Port Aransas and walk the miles of beach and, without a doubt, you will find the remains of at least one sand castle. The majority of visitors seem to feel the call of the sand to create their own medieval masterpiece. Some even get so serious as to call a local sand castle builder for some lessons.

But at no time do the number of sand castles and other fanciful creations reach the peak as during Texas Sandfest (texassandfest.org), the annual competition on the beach here that attracts over 300 sculptors.

And if there's anything the artists really hate, it's a beer-drinker who likes to kick things over—that, and high water.

That's why event organizers pick a date that avoids busy weekends and waves.

"It's either March or April, and it's determined by the tide," said Dee McElroy, former SandFest director. "We avoid Easter; we avoid spring break; we avoid the summer rush. So within that narrow window we check a year in advance. It has to be the lowest tide so we can have the beaches wider and there's no threat to the sculptures."

One of the best-known artists goes by the name of sandy feet (small s, small f). Ms. feet, whose real name is Lucinda Wierenga (so you can see why she might change her name to feet), is a regular entrant. A master sand sculptor from South Padre Island, sandy feet is a prime example of why SandFest selects its dates so carefully. Several years ago one of her works was the victim of a storm, which raised the water level at the beach and took out one of her artworks. "It just kind of melted," McElroy recalled.

Ms. feet was on her toes, though, and managed to turn a bad situation into a humorous, yet sandy, tour de force. "Well, I had started off building just a big castle, but after the destruction occurred, I carved a spring-breaker flailing around in the middle of the castle and it had a bunch of empty beer

Yep, another vacationer has tried his hand at sand sculpting.
PARIS PERMENTER AND JOHN BIGLEY

cans," feet recalled. "And I titled it *Irresistible Force Meets Immovable Object*. So it turned out okay."

That sort of thing is all in a day's work for sand castle makers. "That's what you've got to do is be creative, because the sand isn't always cooperative," said feet, who has a book out called *Sand Castles Made Simple*. "You have to go to Plan B and sometimes Plan C. And Plan C is almost always a sea turtle."

SandFest's sculptors enter in two categories: amateur and masters. From the latter group you'll see all sorts of intricate and amazing artworks made of sand and water, some of them as high as about twelve feet: Pope John Paul in his robes and his tall pope hat, three curious monkeys (one with a mike, one with earphones, the third looking through binoculars), a sand likeness of the tapestry that shows the dogs sitting around a table playing poker.

"A lot of them do people, a lot of them do architectural buildings like castles, some go for the real whimsical approach, which is a real crowd pleaser," McElroy said. "Some have more profound sculptures, conveying a message. Some are more artsy in their approach."

Farley Boats
Port Aransas

Drive through Port A and you'll see small boats acting as planters in front of area businesses, parks, and homes. You might think they're just cute miniatures that provide a spot of color—but, in fact, they're pint-sized homages to the famed Farley Boats of Port Aransas.

Created by Charles Frederick ("Fred") Farley, the Farley boat was designed specifically for the tarpon anglers in Port Aransas. The first Farley boats were 18 to 22 feet long with a high bow to handle the chop of the Gulf waters.

The boats drew the attention of the world when FDR came to Port Aransas to fish in 1937. The president tried his hand at tarpon fishing from his own boat, with no luck. Farley's brother, Barney, took FDR out in a Farley Boat and the excursion was so successful that FDR returned for another fishing trip the next year.

Today Farley Boat Works (portaransasmuseum.org; 716 W. Avenue C) still conducts boat building classes. Farley Boat Works and the Port Aransas Museum took a devastating hit from Hurricane Harvey in the summer of 2017, but have since reopened, though there is still a lot of work ahead to make a full recovery. Youth Boat Build Camp has been scheduled for June 2018.

You can't throw a seashell in Port Aransas without hitting one of the many Farley boat-inspired planters. PARIS PERMENTER AND JOHN BIGLEY

The Shark at the Door
Port Aransas and South Padre Island

The Texas coast is home to more than one Jaws, big, artistic, faux fish with a pink tongue and lots of teeth. In other words, to enter these stores you have to become bait. Some might find it tacky, but it's probably a step up from the big sign in the souvenir shop window next door that says, LADIES SWIMSUITS 60 PERCENT OFF.

This toothy fellow serves as a photo op at Port Aransas's Destination Beach and Surf. PARIS PERMENTER AND JOHN BIGLEY

The shark entrances provide a popular photo opportunity for tourists. People are constantly driving up to the front of the store and taking a picture of it. Grab your camera and dive in at these toothy stops:

- Destination Beach and Surf, 516 S Alister St, Port Aransas
- Third Coast Beach Company, 14501 S Padre Island Dr, Corpus Christi
- Palace Beachwear and Gifts, 3017 N Shoreline Blvd, Corpus Christi
- Jaws, 815 Padre Blvd, South Padre Island

The Tarpon Inn
Port Aransas

If you want to see tarpon scales, stay at this old hotel (thetarponinn.com; 200 East Cotter, 361-749-5555), which opened in 1886 and was listed in the National Register of Historic Places in 1979.

Tarpon fishing and a visit by FDR put Port Aransas on the map.

PARIS PERMENTER AND JOHN BIGLEY

It's been a tradition over the years to take a scale from the tarpon you caught, write your name, your hometown, and the size of the fish (if it's worth bragging about) on it, and affix it to the wall in the lobby.

As you walk into the lobby, the right wall is entirely covered with these signed tarpon scales. Penny Jones, the former desk clerk, said she heard there are about 3,500 fish scales in all. You can read the scales on the wall and see who caught what. J. C. Blackwood of Midland caught a six-foot-seven-incher on June 9, 1950. Ginnie Hills of Bloomfield Hills, Michigan, caught a five-foot-three-inch tarpon on July 17, 1946. Franklin Delano Roosevelt caught a five-foot-one-inch tarpon on May 8, 1937. Because FDR was president, his scale rates a frame on the back wall, along with a couple of photos of him landing the fish.

The Tarpon Inn is a quaint, old barracks-shaped building. You can sit on the long front porch in a rocker and hear the fishing boats in the waterway.

Damaged by Hurricane Harvey in the summer of 2017, the Inn closed but reopened April 25, 2018.

World's Largest Fly Rod and Reel
Port Isabel

An avid fly fisherman, the late Tiney Mitchell would attribute his building of the 71 foot, 4½ inch long fly rod to opening his mouth at a directors' meeting of the Laguna Madre Fly Fishing Association.

"When the guys got done batting the breeze about how they could get some publicity and get some people to come down here from Dallas and Houston to fish with us, I opened my mouth and said, 'I know what. Let's build the world's largest fly rod and reel,'" said Tiney, "And of course I was appointed a committee of one."

At first Tiney and his next-door neighbor and buddy, Leroy Addison, who helped with the project, intended to build the rod out of aluminum flag poles. But the *Guinness World Records* folks said that wouldn't work because it wouldn't be authentic.

"When we got the letter from *Guinness*, we had to back off and go to fiberglass," Tiney said. Leroy found a company in Wichita, Kansas, that manufactures fiberglass tubing. The company donated the material for the rod. So Leroy and Tiney built the rod—as well as the big tarpon—in Leroy's driveway.

A big fish can be seen leaping out of the water just off Pirate's Landing Fishing Pier here. It is arranged in such a way that it looks as though it is about to be hooked by the gigantic fly rod, which is set up next to the fishing pier building. "The tarpon is twenty feet long, and its mouth is wide open and the fly is out in front of it," Tiney said. "It appears the tarpon is jumping out of the water after a fly."

"It's made out of fiberglass sheeting," Leroy said of the fish. "We took marine plywood and made the backbone; then we made the ribs out of two-by-two wood."

The project began in 1997, and the fly rod—now certified by *Guinness* as the world's largest—was erected in 1999. The reel is four feet in diameter, and like everything else on this rod, it's to scale and it works.

The operation of the fly rod would require the combined strength of two dozen strong men or one large Texan, according to the sign in front of the fly rod. By the way, Tiney spent a lot of his own money on the project. But he wasn't sure how much. His wife kept the books and she wouldn't tell him.

Janis Joplin's School Daze
Port Arthur

Yes, the 1960s rock singer with the ballsy voice actually had a slide rule in high school. And if it wasn't for Sam Monroe, former president of the Port Arthur Historical Society and Lamar State College, Port Arthur, you might not be able to see it.

In the 1980s, Monroe, who went to Thomas Jefferson High in Port Arthur with Joplin, led the drive to get a Joplin exhibit going. Today, you'll find it in the Music Hall in the Museum of the Gulf Coast, 700 Procter St., Port Arthur (museumofthegulfcoast.org; 409-982-7000).

Monroe said he had some trouble getting the job done. Some people in town didn't think honoring Joplin, who died of a drug overdose at twenty-seven, was a good idea "because of her lifestyle and the manner in which she died," he admitted. "But we made the case with the people that her career was so significant that she should be recognized."

Along with Joplin's slide rule, you'll find Janis Joplin's senior yearbook, awards Janis won for outstanding achievement in art and English at Wood-row Wilson Junior High, a birthday note fourteen-year-old Janis wrote to her mother to invite her to dinner at Luby's, one of her performing outfits done by Nudie of Hollywood, even a replica of Janis Joplin's ragtop Porsche; it has a big smiling sun on the back end and is quite psychedelic.

Monroe knew Joplin fairly well. They went to kindergarten together, graduated from Thomas Jefferson High School in 1960 together, and though they didn't date, they did double-date.

"Janis was multidimensional," Monroe said. "I think she was a little bit ahead of her time." She was not a follower. There was an all-gal drum and bugle corps in high school called the Red Hussars.

"Every female student wanted to be in the Red Hussars," Monroe said—except Janis. "She had a large cadre of friends, but she did not want to be part of the mainstream."

Really Big Tree
Near Rockport

Located at Goose Island State Park off TX 35, about twelve miles north of Rockport, the Goose Island Oak, certified as the State Champion Coastal Live Oak, is a panhandler. Over 1,000 years old, the tree—with a trunk circumference of 36 feet—hits people up for spare change.

It does this with the assistance of a corny poem—perhaps I should say "acorny poem"—displayed on a sign near the tree. Next to the sign is a Texas Parks and Wildlife Department donation box.

The Goose Island Oak is appropriately named "Big Tree".
PARIS PERMENTER AND JOHN BIGLEY

Here's some of this sappy poem:
"Yet through all the seasons, sorrows, bitterness and beauty
All of the history I have withstood and witnessed,
There had been one thing I could not do.
I could not grow dollars, or silver or gold.
Will you help me, standing here before me?
Then we both may grow old, together.
As old friends should.
One of flesh, one of wood."
Get a job. Actually, in a weak moment I gave the tree 50 cents.

I like the wooden sign set in the ground in front of the tree. It says, simply, BIG TREE. Well, no kidding! You could start a furniture store with this thing.

World's Largest Blue Crab
Rockport

Feeling crabby? The world's largest blue crab just might put a smile on your face, if for no other reason than the gender bending artistic license that has been taken with this fiberglass fellow.

There's nothing to be crabby about in Rockport. PARIS PERMENTER AND JOHN BIGLEY

Rockport long had a blue crab sculpture, constructed in the 1950s. Time and weather eventually took its toll on the crustacean, though—but the people of Rockport still yearned for a giant crab. The painter who did some touchup work on that original crab painted the red claws of female blue crab on the body of a male crab. When sculptor David Allgood was commissioned to create today's giant blue crab from fiberglass and aluminum, he kept his design true to that original look.

This hermaphrodite sculpture stood at the entrance of Rockport Beach Park (rockportbeach-texas.com; 210 Seabreeze Dr.) but was nearly destroyed by Hurricane Harvey in August 2017. Plans call for the crab to eventually be rebuilt and once again greet visitors to the beach park.

Tee Pee Motel & RV Park
Wharton

Once upon a time during the golden era of roadside novelties, tepee (or wigwam) tourist courts could be found all along America's roadsides. Today, only four remain in the United States. The Tee Pee Motel & RV Park in Wharton (teepeemotelandrvpark.com; 3699 N. Richmond Rd., 979-282-8474) is the only surviving one in Texas. The others are wigwams in Arizona, California, and Kentucky. So you can still trade wampum for a night in a tepee.

Designed in 1942 by George and Toppie Belcher, the eleven tepees weren't actually built until after WW II because of supply rationing. Contractor Lacy Helms had a heck of a time plodding through red tape to obtain permission from the government to get enough lumber to build the framework for the tepees. The tepees were a huge success and popular for decades. They changed hands a few times and were finally abandoned in the 1980s . . . until 2004.

With their lottery winnings, new owners have given the tepees new life, saying they wanted to preserve this piece of American history. Beautifully renovated, each of the spacious units has a comfortable bedroom and private bath. You'll even find a coffee maker, microwave, and refrigerator. Decor portrays Native American history, and no two are alike. The complex also includes an RV park with full hookups.

And they say gambling is a bad thing.

A classic motel recalls the golden age of road travel. TEE PEE MOTEL & RV PARK.

Index

Z

About the Authors

John Kelso was a humor columnist with the *Austin American-Statesman* in Austin, Texas, from 1977 and well through his 2011 retirement, publishing his last column just a few weeks before he passed away from complications with a second bout of cancer in 2017. He received an award for humor writing in 2005 from the National Press Club. He lived in South Austin with his wife, Kay; daughter, Rachel; dogs Harry, Ziggy, and Belle; cats Bitsy, Nutmeg, Oreo, and Scooter; and a bunch of other neighbor cats who hang out in the garage.

Paris Permenter and John Bigley are a husband-wife team of travel writers who make their home in the Hill Country west of Austin. In addition to writing for many magazines and newspapers, they have written numerous guidebooks, including *Insiders' Guide® to San Antonio*, *Day Trips® from Austin*, and *Day Trips® from Houston*.